the sweet truth

a sugar-free/wheat-free kitchen

by kelly e. keough

ISBN

the sweet truth

1-4196-6177-9

disclaimer

This book is sold for information purposes only. Neither the author nor the publisher will be held accountable for the use or misuse of the information contained in this book. This book is not intended as medical advice, because the author and publisher of this work are not medical doctors and to not recommend the use of medicines to achieve relief from ailments associated with sugar and wheat.

The author, publisher, and distributor of this book are not responsible for and adverse effects or consequences resulting from the use of any recipes, suggestions, or procedures described hereafter.

dedication

This self-help cookbook is dedicated to everyone who has ever healed the Self and continues to do so, for this book is a blueprint for personal healing from sugar addiction and compulsive overeating using the tool of food as inspiration. The healing for me is an ongoing process and journey of discovery that has no destination, diet plan, or number on a scale, just a clear path of ascension rooted in optimal health and a pleasurable and joyful relationship with the sweets that I eat.

This cookbook is dedicated to my mother. She taught me how to cook. And also to my great grandmother, Louise Schwert, a private cook for the rich who lived on Lake Erie. Gran hand wrote all her own recipes in a notebook and that notebook became her cookbook that has been passed down from generation to generation. I took three of Gran's recipes and transposed them Sweet Truth style into sugar-free/wheat-free desserts (Cry Babies, Gran's Strawberry Rhubarb Pie, and Mocha Maca Crumb Cake). I wish Gran would have known then what I know now about sugar-free alternatives, because she died of diabetes without even knowing she had the disease. Diabetes runs in my family. Because of this, every day I make a consistent decision to satisfy my sweet tooth with low glycemic dishes and desserts and do the exercise that I love: ballet, salsa, yoga, and surfing.

This book is especially dedicated to my grandmother, Eleanor Chiavetta of Chiavetta's Catering in Brant, NY, (better know as Nana). From the time I was born she always told me I could be anything I want to be – and let me tell you, being a sugar-free chef was the furthest thing from my mind. In fact, there really was no such thing at all when she would sing that hopeful mantra to me as I went off to summer day camp with my sacred grape soda.

Sip. Sip. Hmm… What do I want to be? I would ask myself this deep question every time my independently-thinking Nana would say those words – though it would soon be muffled out of ear shot as I indulged in yet more sugar.

So how did I get from there to here? That's another cookbook, but I did have a tell-tale dream that warned me I would never "make it" in Hollywood if I didn't give up sugar. I guess that warning from my inner guidance wasn't strong enough for me to put down the white stuff. No, it took ample hair loss and the threat of balding at 39 years of age to hit home the fact that my body was out of balance. Once sugar was now out of the picture , I finally came into focus.

I am eternally grateful to share this information with you.

the sweet truth the sweet truth
the sweet truth the sweet truth
the sweet truth the sweet truth
the sweet truth the sweet truth
the sweet truth the sweet truth
the sweet truth the sweet truth
the sweet truth the sweet truth
the sweet truth the sweet truth
the sweet truth the sweet truth
the sweet truth the sweet truth
the sweet truth the sweet truth
the sweet truth the sweet truth
the sweet truth the sweet truth
the sweet truth the sweet truth
the sweet truth the sweet truth

intro

Would you like to be free of sugar? And wheat, too? If so, what would being free of sugar and wheat look like, feel like,and most importantly, taste like? And if you do want to cook and bake sugar-free/wheat-free, where do you go shopping? Just where do you begin? The answers to these questions are the keystones that gave me the inspiration, courage, and commitment it takes to go on the sweet truth path of transformation, healing, and health through a sugar-free/wheat-free food practice. But it's easier than you think. With just one recipe like FUDGE IT, a 90 second gourmet truffle, I changed my life. You can too. This self-help cookbook has offers a sugar-free/wheat-free cooking style and food philosophy that allows you to have your sweets and eat them too, and reap the benefits from this innovative healthy and delicious lifestyle.

First, sugar-free/wheat-free looks great on your body -- inside and out. It increases the beauty and glow of your skin, hair, and face. By removing the inflammatory properties of white sugar and flour from your food plan and replacing them with sugar-free/wheat-free alternatives, not only can you reduce water retention, weight gain, premature wrinkles, poor digestion, a depressed immune system, and symptoms of overall aging, you can still have your sweets and eat them too, without the guilt. Also, the most vital plus we can gain from being sugar-free/wheat-free is keeping our blood sugar levels as even as possible, and therefore, our hormone levels as well. This is the very first transition you will notice. You will look and feel more beautiful, weigh less, and feel happy.

The second benefit of being sugar-free/wheat-free answers the question, "What does it feel like?" I just mentioned it feels happy, really happy. It also feels beautiful. Beyond happy and beautiful, it feels real. Really calm, peaceful, grounded, healthy, clear, steady, and non-addictive. For me, being sugar-free/wheat-free feels absolutely free. Free to show up for myself, breathe deeply, and discover the more of me, and that feels awesome.

It is also a miracle what I don't feel. I don't feel out of control around sugar, the urge to eat a bag of cookies is no more, and the compulsion around food is now a healthy impulse to nourish myself with sound and tasty nutrition that feeds my body and my spirit and still looks and tastes like a chocolate chip cookie. You just can't take away a kid's craving for a cookie. Or a woman like me for that matter.

Now, the crucial question of taste. After eating one of my desserts, people say in amazement, "That has no sugar?" Truth is, it doesn't. None at all. The third and ultimate reward of cooking and eating sugar-free/wheat-free is the sweet and satisfying taste without the ill effects of sugar: headache, bloat, dull and blemished skin, spiked blood sugar levels and hormonal imbalances. You have to taste it to believe it. Some of the recipes in this book are super sweet and some are not. Try a recipe out and give yourself the taste bud challenge. Not all taste buds are made the same. Most have been trained for years to enjoy all the wicked whites: sugar, salt, flour, and creamy butter. Mine have definitely transformed into desiring healthy and naturally sweet tasting foods through the process of becoming free of sugar. White sugar now tastes like a chemical and not a food. Using diabetic-safe and natural sweeteners like agave nectar tastes better to me than honey, replaces the liquid component of sugar in baking, and has a low glycemic index. How can that not taste great?

Now that you know you don't have to live without sweets and that the alternative ingredients to sugar and wheat can be used to heal your body and satisfy your sweet tooth -- where do you get the goods? And how do you begin?

Weekly planning and preparation with a menu and food shopping list are your best tools for success. Once your list is hand, you can visit your local health food store like Erewhon in Los Angeles, a specialty macrobiotic store that I showcased on my TV cooking show, THE SWEET TRUTH on Veria TV, or a natural food store like Whole Foods Market that carries all natural and organic produce and products and is committed to only selling products that are free of chemicals, trans fats, and pollutants. If they don't carry an item, you can always ask customer service to special order it for you. Also listed in the cookbook is on-line ordering information. Getting your sugar-free/wheat-free pantry stocked is a breeze, making your first recipe is fun, and discovering the sweet truth -- your true identity -- with the support of a sugar-free/wheat-free food philosophy and practice is so satisfying. And that's because...

the sweet truth is YOU!

contents

the sweet truth

the sweet truth pantry

recipes

the sweet truth

a sugar-free/wheat-free cooking style and food philosophy

The Sweet Truth is a breakthrough food practice that heals sugar and flour addiction, increases self-esteem, and allows you to have your sweets and eat them, too. "Great," you say. "But will I lose weight?" Definitely.

The magic key to health and beauty is to keep the blood sugar level even by not eating white sugar and wheat flour. Both are high in glucose and raise insulin levels in the blood, causing fat storage. Replace them with the Tools of Nature: agave nectar, stevia, quinoa, and buckwheat.

Sugar and flour are highly allergenic and slow down digestion; if you are gluten intolerant, both may stop absorption of vitamins and minerals. Therefore, increase your nutrient-dense foods like seaweed and organic leafy greens as well. Increase digestive fires and stimulate metabolism and reduce inflammation with spices like cinnamon and turmeric. And cook! Cook! Cook!

Also, weigh and measure your meals along with the amount of stress you take in and give out. Pray that each meal is enough food and always know there will be another.

Most of all, still eat dessert without stimulating your compulsion for overeating! Sweetness is the essence of life and opens the gateway for you to experience your true identity. Meet your culinary destiny as I have met mine. It starts in the kitchen.

But above all, live and love your one and only own sweet truth.

my story, a little story...

Terrible Two. That's the label with which we adults lovingly anoint a small person of 24 months who has hasn't quite figured out that there are other people on this planet besides themselves.

Only two and already terrible. Yet this is the name I gave myself at the tender age of 730 days as I stood barefoot on the cold, dark-spotted linoleum bathroom floor of my grandmother's house in western New York. It was my home away from home and the center of "Chiavetta's Barbeque Chicken and Catering Business," famous for taste. For me, it provided too much easy backstage access to food. Down at my belly I stared, dressed in a yellow bikini, and said, "C'est terrible!" Well, I couldn't speak French yet, but if I could, that's what I would have said.

How can a child at the age of two understand the concept of "fat"? Call me an intuitive baby, but I did, and I knew. I was a chubby bubby. And I didn't like it. From that moment on, I hated myself and my body, never mind the yellow polka-dot bikini that only looks good on dolls.

I guess I could have blamed it all on the BBQ chicken that was available to me on a 24-7 basis, but let's face it. The truth is, it was the lemon filled sheet cakes. Or was it the strawberry with chocolate frosting? I'll eat cake over chicken any day. And that's what I did growing up in a Sicilian family with a catering business. I ate cake and lots of it! But I do blame my grandmother for putting me on the cake service line instead of the chicken when I worked for their catering business every summer since the age of 14. How else was I supposed to keep the spatula clean?

It's been 40 years since then...

a different story

Addicted to sugar? Who isn't? I can honestly say I was and I am not anymore. And I healed from this terrible disease through my sugar-free/wheat-free food practice. I didn't go without, I ate better than I ever have and had desserts without guilt. Did I lose weight? Yes, and for the first time in my life, without trying. I no longer diet, I plan food -- or in other words, I have a food plan that satisfies my sweet tooth. Believe me, at first it was daunting and yet I dared myself to put myself back into balance. I was desperate to recover the third of my hair that had fallen out due to chronic emotional and nutritional stress. The message I gave myself was that

I had to heal, not lose weight. And that's ultimately how I lost weight. I focused instead on being sugar-free/wheat-free. The same can happen to you. You can lose weight, look great, and have shiny strong hair all with the Sweet Truth cooking style and food philosophy. Not a diet but a new practice... Guilt-free sweet recipes, from breakfast to dessert, for radiant beauty and easy weight loss using diabetic safe agave, Stevia, and other natural foods that are low-glycemic sweeteners in conjunction with good fats, fiber, and protein to keep blood sugar levels balanced and properly fed.

Rooted in organic, whole foods and excluding all refined white sugar and wheat flour, the recipes in this self-help cookbook also use sweet fruits and vegetables, and gluten-free whole grains like quinoa, buckwheat, sorghum flour, and garbanzo bean flour. It's great for people on low-glycemic diets, those with diabetes II, hypoglycemia, or celiac disease. I created this practice to re-grow my hair and balance my hormonal system and was given so much more. I discovered more of who I am. By stripping away the sugar and flour, I uncovered the more of me. Now, I love to wear bathing suits.

Low-carb diets are good for some people, but not for me and definitely not for you if you want to enjoy what life has to offer. And that is sweetness with a low glycemic index and lots of nutrition. But that doesn't mean I go off and eat what I want whenever I want. I eat one cup or 1/2 cup servings or 2 cookies at a time because I believe a balanced body, mind, and spirit equal the trinity of beauty, truth, and clear perception of the self. And I think myself a queen.

Whether Marie Antoinette said it or not, "Let them eat cake!" is a command I am eagerly willing to obey. Why? Because as I call the officially self-proclaimed Queen of Quinoa, I know how to eat cake and still lose the weight without the guilt because I bake with high protein, gluten-free quinoa flour. I even know how to answer the number one question posed by people starting off on a new and exotic food adventure, "What do I eat for breakfast?" The answer? Something sweet, delicious, and satiating with high protein and a low glycemic index so you're not feeling deprived by 10:00 am.

So if you want to lose the first 50 pounds (like I did) or the last twelve pounds that haven't come off in the last ten years (which I finally did lose), and you want to get off sugar and flour and yet are afraid to, then this cookbook is for you. I promise, you'll find a recipe that works for you and your family, and still satisfies your sweet tooth.

the sweet truth principles

planning

preparation

prayer

planning

Start with one simple recipe like a dessert. Make a grocery list of the items you don't already have in your pantry. Plan a trip to your local natural food store or shop on the internet, (I have included websites under the online shopping section of the cookbook). Make it. Eat it. Notice the difference in how it makes you feel. Great! You're ready to build your Sweet Truth pantry.

The next step starts with a full grocery list containing my Sweet Truth pantry staples. Here are a few of my favorites to get you started: agave, Stevia, carob, cinnamon, unsweetened carob chips, unsweetened almond milk, unsalted raw tahini, all purpose gluten-free flour, xanthan gum, quinoa grains, nori and sea vegetables, and yams. You can always buy sea vegetables like hijiki, kombu, kanten, and wakame online, at your local Asian market, or at your local natural food store. All of the ingredients in this cookbook can bought at natural food stores like Whole Foods and Wild Oats, and at your local organic health food store like Erewhon in Los Angeles.

After the grocery list is complete, I plan five sweet or sweet and savory dishes in the following categories: dessert, grain, root veggie,green veggie, and a lentil or bean dish. All the recipes in my cookbook were designed to guarantee that you will have more sweet tooth satisfaction throughout the day and will be less likely to crave and eat white sugar and flour. It may take three to six months to completely lose your desire for white sugar, but it does happen. It is a practice and a process, so use the desserts wisely. I found making them at least once a week (sometimes twice a week) for the first six months really helped me heal my body from craving white sugar and flour. Then I tapered off to every other week and all special occasions. What I kept very consistent on a day to day basis was the root veggie dishes like yams for sweetness and long lasting carbs that break down slowly in the blood stream.

For protein, I eat eggs, chicken, turkey, fish, and tofu on occasion. I also ate dessert every day and I maintained my weight after I lost it. I found after my sugar cravings left me, so did my desire for dessert all the time. So the best rule of thumb is, if you crave it, make it. But make sure it's sugar-free/wheat-free and guilt-free. It's more important to listen to your body, mind, and spirit. Give it what it needs in the form of a satisfying and healthy treat. This will re-pattern your inner and outer reactions to food. It will also aid in balancing your entire system. If you don't appease your sweet tooth craving, be it physical or emotional, you will deprive yourself, eat something you don't care for and may end up binge eating extra or unwanted refined white sugar and flour. That's what I found repeatedly happened to me. That is why it is so important to PLAN AHEAD.

preparation

Writing a grocery list and dreaming about what you are going to eat helps you to use your imagination and is a lot of fun, especially when you know you are going to make and eat a guilt-free and satisfying dessert. Making a list helps me commit to my healing process on a weekly basis. Creative and committed consistency is the key to success of any practice. In this case, it's a sugar-free/wheat-free food practice. If I didn't heal my stress, remove sugar and flour from my food plan, and balance my system, I'd go bald. It was that simple. I was ready to commit. This health problem completely put me in the moment. I watched everything I put in my mouth. Within two weeks, people where commenting on my glowing skin and my effortless weight loss. I was changing my looks through food. I was also changing the way I felt about myself on the inside. This gave me the self-esteem and motivation to go forward.

Now that you have a grocery list, the next step to taking preparation to the next level is to plan a three-hour block of time each week to make the five dishes I already mentioned. Then have fun. Cooking in the kitchen like this will burn over 400 calories. I look at it as an opportunity for exercise. It's also a time to infuse your own healing energy into your cooking and think positively about yourself. Instant therapy! That's what I call it and it only costs the price of food. I get many good ideas to solve problems when I am in the kitchen, and it's also my great escape from the pressures of living in Los Angeles and being away from my family and best friends in Massachusetts.

The relatively short time it takes to plan a grocery list that in three hours will turn out four sugar-free/wheat-free satisfying meals and a dessert on a weekly basis is a very rewarding and grounding activity. It can be done with a best friend, family members, or solo. Either way, planning and preparation yields success for an optimum healthy lifestyle that is enjoyable and tastes better than it ever did.

If I didn't cook, I'd lose my mind, and gain lots of weight. Preparation through planning and cooking has given me the gift of the goddess -- it has put me in touch with my deep creative resources and connection to myself and others by being able to nurture myself through my Sweet Truth food practice. I love myself more for it. And it is all because of releasing (really surrendering) sugar and flour from my life. This last sentence brings me to the third and most powerful principal of all: PRAYER.

prayer

I just mentioned how cooking for people is a grounded and sensual show of love, and being loved in return, especially if the dish tastes amazing and satisfying. And isn't this reminiscent of Mother? Mother is the one who fed us, or didn't feed us. As adults, Mother Earth feeds us now by growing food sources for us, and yes, she even grows sugar cane, but she also grows agave and stevia. Mother knows we need sweets. Sweet is a metaphor for love and love is what we all want and crave.

When I feel I don't get enough love, I tend to overeat - and this is where the praying comes in. Every time I eat I pray, "God, let this be enough food and let me know there will always be another meal." Sometimes for me, satisfying my sweet tooth with a no-guilt, sugar-free, wheat-free dessert is not enough. Intuiting the amount that is perfect for my body must be a part of my Sweet Truth practice. Let me repeat. This is a practice. Every meal is a new opportunity to be in alignment with my inner balance of beauty, truth, and perception. Since I was a compulsive overeater, I use a measuring cup. I believe in eating to satisfy, especially when beginning a new food plan. Then as your body loses weight and balances all it's systems, you will need less food naturally. Ultimately you will come to know that you are loved. Always. It took me 42 years to figure that out. But even when I was in the dark about this, I diligently executed my food practice, I measured my food and found that because I wasn't eating sugar I wasn't triggering my sugar addiction. I naturally began to eat suggested serving sizes like two small cookies for dessert.

Measuring is just as much a technical exercise as it is a spiritual exercise. Being aware of the amount of stress you are taking on is just as important as monitoring the amount of food you are taking in. Less stress is less opportunity to overeat. Here are some guidelines for measuring. At first, start out with the one cup rule. One cup grains, beans or lentils, sautéed veggies or root vegetable or dessert. After three months, or when your body naturally tells you to cut back, go to 3/4 of a measuring cup and then to a 1/2 cup. Don't fret. When you have the last 5-10 pounds to lose like me, it's enough food. That's what my body tells me. This is the reward or "fruit" of the Sweet Truth practice - that your ability to use your body as an intuitive tool for healing becomes more apparent.

Releasing sugar and wheat flour from your system, along with other toxins, will give you the ability to be present in your body and listen to its wisdom. Couple this with yoga, meditation, exercise you love, and a sugar-free, wheat-free nutrient-dense food practice and you are on your way to freedom. To dream like you never did before. Therefore, praying becomes second nature. Remember to do it at each meal. What will start to happen is your body will tell you how much to measure, what ingredients are good for you, and what you're allergic to even before you eat. Actually, your body already does this. Once you start the practice, you will start to listen. And isn't that what you want God to do when you pray?

tools of nature

Now that you know the tips, here are the tools. On the pages that follow are the list of tools I use on a consistent basis. They include: the staples, a shopping list, if you're craving this - eat that list, sample menus, information on Stevia, buckwheat, quinoa, and sea vegetables, and of course, the recipes. These tools would be useless if it were not for the healing properties of nature found in food. The Tools of Nature are the backbone to the success of practicing "The Sweet Truth". These Tools of Nature also include fresh, organic whole fruits and vegetables, herbs, spices, and teas.

These building blocks balance your system by boosting vitality, increasing metabolism, increasing digestion and absorption, tuning the hormonal system, evening out mood and mental outlook, and detoxify and ward off free radicals which leave the body, mind and spirit clear and free. You can't help but raise your self-esteem. Here's to your culinary destiny!

the sweet truth pantry

sugar-free

wheat-free

gluten-free

dairy-free

setting up your sugar-free pantry

Sweet and diabetic-safe, my main sweetener is agave nectar. Organic light and dark agave are made from the succulent blue weber agave, a cactus like plant grown in Mexico. Agave is a very affordable super-healthy sugar alternative and found in most health food stores. It replaces my honey and is used in my baking as a liquid sugar. The blue weber agave plant makes many products, the most popular of which is tequila, but that's only if the agave plant is grown in the Jalisco region of Mexico. The long 10-12 foot leaves of the agave are cut off and the pina, the bottom stem of the plant which is attached to the root but above ground, is harvested. The juice from the pina is squeezed out and through a cooking process made into nectar or honey.

It's important to know that the blue weber agave is the only agave plant to produce a nectar that is diabetic-safe. Other species of agave plants may have different fructose levels and not be beneficial for people who desire to watch their sugar intake. Organic blue weber agave grows abundantly in many regions of Mexico, not just in Jalisco. Legend has it that there was a goddess, Mayahuel, who was a trickster. Another ruling god did not approve of her flirtatious ways, chopped off her head, and cut her into tiny pieces. The farmers and people of the town loved Mayahuel so much, they buried her body all over the land. Mayahuel resurrected herself through the great love of the people and grew back as an abundant succulent, agave. Now everyone can taste her fruits.

Liquid and powdered stevia is produced by a green leafed plant from Paraguay, and oligofructose and erythritol, trademarked as Zeratol, is made from fruit and vegetable fiber. These are my main sugar-free sweeteners and they are always stocked in my Sweet Truth pantry.

These sweeteners are all natural and made with no chemicals. What I don't use -- natural or not -- is high fructose corn syrup, fructose crystals, maple syrup, corn syrup, turbinado, brown rice syrup, honey, molasses, organic cane or brown sugar, xylitol, sorbitol, manitol, Splenda, or Nutra Sweet. Those sweeteners make me bloated, gain weight, compulse on more sugar, and give my diarrhea and headaches.

Agave and stevia are not fake sugars like Splenda or NutraSweet, nor are they sugar alcohols like Xylitol, Sorbitol, and Malitol. Sugar alcohols are expensive, don't bake correctly, and adversely affect my body and digestive system. But the primary reason I don't use these types of sweeteners is because I want to keep my blood sugar level even and stable as possible. I carefully chose the best, all-natural and organic sweeteners I could find that have no glycemic index at all like stevia and zeratol or a very low glycemic index like diabetic-safe agave to keep my body and sugar cravings in balance.

What is a glycemic index?

All carbohydrate foods like bread, cookies, yams, carrots, or quinoa are not created equal. They each affect my body differently. If I eat a yam, I feel great and have no ill side effects. If I eat an Oreo Cookie, I want to eat ten more (even thought I don't anymore), but even after one, I feel the ill affects of a sharp rise in my blood sugar. This is especially true now that I have been free of sugar for over three years.

According to the University of Sydney, the glycemic index (or GI) describes this difference in food by ranking carbohydrates according to their effect on our blood glucose levels. Choosing low GI carbs -- the ones that produce only small fluctuations in our blood glucose and insulin levels -- is the secret to my long-term health, losing weight and keeping it off, looking young, reducing pain in my body, reducing wrinkles, slowing the aging process, as well as protecting my most treasured organ, my heart. Low GI foods helped heal my body and now I want to keep myself young, healthy, beautiful, and in balance. This is important to me because I would like to have a baby in a few years.

I suffered from childhood obesity. Now childhood obesity and diabetes is an US epidemic. The great news is that mothers can now use agave and stevia to make diabetic-safe treats that will help aid in the battle of these childhood diseases. I wish my mother had known how to make a sugar-free/wheat-free chocolate chip cookie when I was a kid. Because if she did, she would have treated me with a happy confection containing a very low glycemic index, high fiber, high protein, and good fat so my body maintained health and balance from head to toe. These are some of the benefits of eating low GI desserts.

Definition of Glycemic Index

Glycemic Index - (GI): The Glycemic Index is a dietary index that's used to rank carbohydrate-based foods. For the sake of this book, I focus on the glycemic index of the sweeteners I use like agave, stevia, and zeratol. The Glycemic Index predicts the rate at which the ingested food will increase blood sugar levels. The glycemic index of carbohydrates ranges from 0 to 100 ranking based on how fast they affect the level of glucose in the bloodstream (commonly referred to as the "blood sugar" level). Glucose, or sugar, has a GI of 100, meaning it enters the bloodstream immediately; this is the reference point against which other foods are compared like white bread with a GI of 80, Splenda 80, agave 11-19, and stevia 0.

What does all this mean? I was desperate to have my sweets and eat them, too, so I created recipes that satisfy my sweet tooth, are made with organic whole grains, fruits, vegetables, and gluten-free flours -- and therefore are high in fiber. Along with that I add good fats, high protein, and low glycemic or no glycemic sweeteners like stevia and agave. When I switched to this type of food plan, I lost weight without trying and ate more desserts a week than I ever did my entire life. That's because this combination of high fiber and protein coupled with good fats and low glycemic sweeteners keep my blood sugar steady and therefore don't make me gain weight.

Of course I exercise almost every day and have since I was 19 years old. I am 42 now at the writing of this book and do the movement I love most: ballet, salsa, yoga, and surfing. I love ballet and yoga for the discipline and salsa and surfing for the cute men.

Even though you won't find white sugar or flour in my kitchen today, I didn't get there over night. Start slowly and see what appeals to you first. It may all seem exotic, but if you have an illness like diabetes and/or obesity, you may just be inspired to try agave at the very least. And agave is very affordable. Here's a list of my sugar-free alternative sweeteners. The best advice I can give you is to check out this list and then look at my TOP TWELVE ingredients .

sweet truth
sugar-free alternatives

light agave

Comes organic and made from the blue weber agave cactus-like plant grown in Mexico. The blue weber agave is the same plant from which tequila is made. Agave is high in fructose rather than glucose, which allows it to be absorbed slowly into the blood stream, avoiding the "rush" often associated with refined sugar. Agave is 50% sweeter than white table sugar and is my replacement for honey. Light agave is cooked the least time and has a GI of 19 and is safe for diabetics. Use one to two teaspoons in a serving.

dark agave

Like its lighter sibling, dark agave is made from the blue weber agave plant grown in Mexico. Dark agave is cooked a longer time, than light agave, and has more minerals and has a GI of about 11. It's also safe for diabetics. Use one to two teaspoons in a serving.

stevia plus powder

Made from the Stevia rebaudina green leafed plant from Paraguay. As a fine white powder, it is known as stevioside, and is usually mixed with an FOS, Fructooligosaccharide, for more volume. This makes stevia plus powder easier to measure for baking. Stevia Plus Powder is my replacement for sugar especially when combined with agave. The benefits of stevia are that it is diabetic safe, calorie free, 300 times sweeter than sugar, and doesn't adversely affect blood sugar. It is also non-toxic, inhibits formation of cavities and plaque, contains no artificial ingredients, and has a zero glycemic index. Comes in packets for easy travel in your purse or in small bulk containers for your pantry.

stevia extract

This is the same as stevia powder minus the FOS. Comes in a very concentrated powdered form and is not recommended for baking, only sweetening drinks.

liquid stevia drops

Made from the Stevia rebaudina green leafed plant from Paraguay. As a fine white powder, it is known as stevioside, but here the stevia is in liquid form and much easier to use in drinks and baking. It can come flavored with all natural flavoring and no alcohol. My top Sweet Truth pantry flavors are Vanilla Creme, Dark Chocolate, Milk Chocolate, Lemon Drops, Cinnamon, and Grape. The benefit of liquid stevia is that it mixes best in drinks and wet baking mixtures. Believe it or not, sugar is considered a wet ingredient in baking and liquid stevia is my sugar replacement, too. I carry Vanilla Creme in my pocketbook at all times and use it at the coffee shop. Another benefit is that you can buy an unflavored liquid stevia and add your own extracts for flavor.

zeratol

Made from fruit and vegetable fiber (oligofructose and erythritol) which undergo an enzymatic process, zeratol is non-toxic, has zero calories and a zero glycemic index, measures like sugar, tastes a lot like sugar,has produces no digestive discomfort, is diabetic-safe, and does not cause tooth decay. One brand name is called Swerve and costs $14.00 for 2 and 1/4 cups, so I use 1/2 cup for most of my recipes and blend the flavors of agave, stevia, spices, and flavorings for the best taste and to extend my Sweet Truth pantry.

yacon - slices, powder, syrup

Comes organic and is scientifically known as Smallanthus sonchifolius. Yacon is a root vegetable from Peru. Yacon roots can be eaten raw and have a pleasant sweetness that comes in part from fructans, carbohydrates that are not metabolized by the human body and therefore can be safely consumed by diabetics. You can buy yacon slices, powder, or syrup on line or at your health food store. Powder is sometimes difficult to find, but slices are usually available, especially on line, so I grind the slices into a powder in my Vita Mix.

carob powder - raw or roasted

A powder or fine flour ground from the carob pod or locust bean. It is a natural sweetener, low in fat, has no caffeine, and is a digestive aid. Its dark brown color and flavor substitutes for chocolate because it has a cocoa-like taste, but lacks the bitterness of chocolate. It comes in two ways, raw carob powder for a milk chocolate flavor or substitute, and roasted carob powder for dark chocolate. I prefer roasted carob for all my recipes. It keeps better as raw carob tends to clump up even when stored in an air tight container.

carob chips, unsweetened

Made from carob powder, non-fat milk, whey powder, palm kernel oil and soy lecithin, so they contain dairy, but no added sugar. They often take the place of chocolate chips in my recipes to avoid extra sugar.

Also, you must check the label, Sunspire carob chips do not guarantee that they are gluten-free. Carob chips don't melt well, but are great in cookies, muffins, scones, or just as a quick snack.

carob chips, dairy-free

Made from carob powder and sweetened with barley malt, these contain no whey or milk but they are definitely not gluten-free.

unsweetened cocoa powder

Made from roasted cocoa nibs. I like to use Valrhona 100 % cocoa powder. It's easy to find and blends well with roasted carob powder. This is a great health tip for adding natural sweetness to your baked goods while cutting down on the caffeine.

unsweetened cocoa baking bars

Many baking bars have added sugar so look for one that is 99% cocoa. I use Scharffen Berger 99% unsweetened baking cocoa bar. It melts well and has a rich dark chocolate flavor.

chocolate chips, grain sweetened

Chocolate chips sweetened with malted barley and corn, but no white sugar like traditional chocolate chips. They are not gluten-free. I sometimes use them with unsweetened carob chips when melting chocolate because carob chips alone don't melt smoothly.

gluten-free chocolate chip substitute

Instead of using grain sweetened chocolate chips, in a double boiler, melt 3 oz 99% dark unsweetened baking chocolate with 1 tablespoon light agave and 1 dropper Liquid Stevia. Whisk in 1 tablespoon unsweetened almond milk. Spread chocolate on baking sheet prepared with wax paper. Chill 30 minutes. Break into pieces and use as chips.

raw cacao nibs

Comes organic and is chocolate in its natural form, a nib, shelled from its pod. Nibs come roasted or raw. Both have a very bitter taste, but the raw nibs are a great way to get a hit of chocolate without the extra added sugar or emulsifiers. Raw cocoa is high in magnesium and aids digestion.

dried fruit

Dates, Coconut date rolls, Raisins, and Figs are all found in my Sweet Truth pantry, especially during holiday time. Even though dried fruit is a high glycemic food, when it is coupled with whole grains, agave, stevia, high fiber, and good fat, the digestion and absorption of the carbohydrates is slower than usual and will not adversely affect my blood sugar.

goji berries and Himalayan Goji Berry juice

Grown primarily in China, the Goji Berry is a not-so-sweet dried red berry know for its high nutritional value: high in vitamin C and amino acids, anti-oxidants, and medicinal qualities for a healthy heart. It can also come in juice form. Many of the juices are blended with other fruit juices to make the flavor more palatable. The dried Goji Berries can be added to granola, trail, mix, smoothies, or eaten by themselves as a quick snack.

fruit concentrates

Comes in a liquid form. I use them sparingly in drinks, mostly for color. They can also be used to naturally color frosting. I use red and purple grape concentrate mostly in this book.

fruit and vegetable powders

Made from fruits like strawberries and raspberries and vegetables like spinach to give flavor and/or color to batters, frostings, or glazes.

sweet truth herbs and spices

I recognized the real power of sweet and savory spices and herbs when I went sugar-free/wheat-free and that's because I had to make everything myself so I could carefully watch what I ate and control what was in the recipe. Using more spices and herbs when I needed to satisfy my taste buds without the extra carb calories, extra sodium and bad fats was paramount to my consistent dedication and love for self-nurture in the kitchen.

Having a "diet mentality" can not only make me feel deprived, it does deprive me and usually leads to malnutrition and bad tasting food devoid of the natural benefits of spices and fresh herbs.

It was when I took my health into my own hands and decided to heal myself through food that I greatly expanded my spice and herb cabinet. Always thinking I had to lose weight made food taste weak and boring, especially if the only methods I used were my George Foreman grill for meats and steamer for vegetables.

Creating sauces, curries, soups, and stews with good fats like grape seed oil, sun flower oil, coconut oil, and extra virgin coconut oil along with spices like cinnamon and garham masala which literally translates into "hot spice" made a world of difference in the taste and satisfaction department. In fact, changing from a diet mentality to a self-nurturing outlook has me eating healthy gourmet every day. I found that completely satisfying my taste buds is the key to balanced eating and sticking to a healthy food plan.

The main spices that I have within reach at all times are cinnamon, turmeric, ginger, cayenne, nutmeg, pumpkin spice, cardamom, clove, apple pie spice, all spice, fennel, garham masala, curry, and Celtic sea salt. I use these spices for their digestive, anti-inflammatory, and metabolism raising benefits.

Consider cinnamon as an everyday spice and sweetener. Cinnamon is an organic spice I always buy in bulk and have at least once a day in a smoothie, cooked cereal, granola, or apple dessert. Cinnamon is known as a sweet spice and a medicine. Not only do I use cinnamon for its satisfying and sweet taste, I use it as an energy elixir when combined with date and carob in many of my Sweet Truth recipes. It has been noted that cinnamon may significantly help people with type II diabetes to improve their ability to respond to insulin and help them normalize their blood sugar levels.

Use turmeric because of its anti-inflammatory properties which produce soft skin and less wrinkles. Turmeric like many other spices is an anti-oxidant which means it stabilizes unstable oxygen molecules which are better known as free radicals. Many of the spices I listed above have been used in Ayurvedic healing.

setting up your wheat-free pantry

I eliminated wheat from my food plan because I wanted better digestion, better absorption of nutrients, healing of my sugar cravings, and weight loss. I wanted to rid myself of all gluten, the gooey protein strand that gives wheat baked goods their height and form. Eliminating wheat and other glutenous grains and flours like barley, rye, spelt, kamut, and oats increased my digestion health and allowed me to loose weight without trying.

In my sugar-free/wheat-free food practice and Sweet Truth recipes, I use gluten-free grains and flours. By eliminating glutenous grains and flours like wheat flour, pasta, and couscous, I found that not only do I have better digestion, less bloating, and feel pain-free with less inflammation in my body, I experienced first hand that I look and feel the best I ever have.

Yet wheat-free does not mean gluten-free. Wheat-free products may still contain other glutenous grains and flours like rye, barley, spelt, kamut, and oats. Oats are sometimes considered glutenous because they have most likely been cross contaminated with close by wheat fields. The majority of the recipes in the Sweet Truth cookbook use gluten-free grains and are gluten-free recipes except in certain recipes where I use oats, grain sweetened chocolate chips, or almond milk which is usually sweetened with brown rice syrup made from malted barley. To substitute oats, use a double amount of puffed brown rice; for any prepared milk alternative like almond milk that has been sweetened with brown rice syrup or malted barley, use unsweetened almond milk or soy milk. For carob chips, check to see that they are unsweetened and completely guaranteed by the manufacturer to be gluten-free.

I have benefited tremendously from eliminating gluten from my food plan by using gluten-free whole grains and flours and at the same time have never felt like I have to live without.

What is Celiac disease and what does gluten-intolerant mean?

People who have Celiac disease or found to be gluten-intolerant have to be careful of all the food and processed food products they consume. Once diagnosed, they have to check with their doctor and get a list of gluten-free foods they can eat and then may be able to add certain grains back into their food plan one at a time. In extreme cases, some of these grains may be millet, buckwheat, or even quinoa which are considered gluten-free.

According to the Celiac Disease Foundation, Celiac disease is defined as a chronic digestive disorder found in individuals that are genetically susceptible, possibly passed on from parent to child. The digestive damage happens in the small intestine where gluten found in products containing wheat, rye, barley, and oats cause a toxic reaction which prevents the nutrients in food to be properly absorbed.

Surprisingly, the following foods contain hidden gluten: dairy-free milks sweetened with brown rice syrup made from malted barley, soups, marinades, soy sauce made from wheat, imitation seafood, and anything made with modified food starch, malt flavoring, and dextrin (usually derived from corn but may be from wheat).

How easy is it to go gluten-free or at least wheat-free?

If you have to have breads, cereals, and baked goods in your food plan (and who doesn't), then you can find gluten-free and wheat-free products pre-made in your health food store. The catch is that they are not sugar-free. That's why the Sweet Truth cookbook was born and the reason I make everything from scratch. My sugar-free/wheat free recipes assure me that I know what I am eating and that I am taking care of my body, mind and spirit. Just the process of making one sugar-free/wheat-free dessert like Fudge It serves as my self-help tool to increase sugar-free satisfaction and increased self-esteem though self-nurture. The most important part of this formula is that it is my path to abstinence from the compulsive overeating of sugar and flour.

Here is a list of wheat-free/gluten-free flours I use in my Sweet Truth pantry.

sweet truth
wheat-free & gluten-free flours

all-purpose gluten-free flour

An all-purpose baking flour made from Garbanzo bean flour, potato starch, tapioca starch, white Sorghum flour, and Fava bean flour. This mix can be bought with or without added leavening ingredients like gluten-free baking powder, soda, and xanthan gum. In all of my Sweet Truth recipes, I use only the all-purpose baking flour and add my own leavening ingredients.

arrow root

The starch, extracted from the rhizomes, is used as a thickener and blends well with gluten-free flours. Interchangeable with cornstarch.

corn starch

Thickener derived from corn.

tapioca starch

Starchy substance extracted from the root of the cassava plant, used mainly in puddings. Tapioca flour is used as a thickener, especially in fruit dishes because it produces a clear gel.

potato flour

Commercially ground from the whole potato, used as a thickener. Retains potato flavor. It looks and feels grainy and is a heavier flour than potato starch.

potato starch

Commercially prepared from cooked potatoes that are washed of all fibers until only the starch remains. Used mostly in my recipes and has the same consistency as tapioca and corn starch. Not the same as potato flour.

quinoa flour and grains

Seed of ancient cereal grain of Peru, related to amaranth. Mild nutty flavor. Versatile; can be substituted for any grain. Used whole as a grain; as a hot cereal; ground into flour. Adds moisture to baked goods.

buckwheat flour and groats

Herb, not a grain and related to rhubarb, with triangular-shaped seed and black shell, used whole in groat form or toasted groat from, cracked or ground into flour.

almond meal

Sweet edible nut used whole or ground into flour. Can be used in combination with other flours, and is used in breads, cakes and pastries.

hazel nut meal

Ground from hazel nuts and may be blended with other flours or used to substitute for almond meal

brown rice flour

Ground form of brown rice with a nutty taste.

white rice flour

Ground form of rice that is gluten-free and non-allergenic. This flour is the best flour to use with spray oiling and flouring your baking pans and rolling out cookie and pizza dough.

sweet sorghum flour

Drought-tolerant cereal grain used primarily as a flour or sweet syrup. Third most prevalent food crop worldwide. Certified food grade white sorghum has been specially developed for the food industry.

corn meal

Maize, cereal plant native to the Americas. Kernels are largest of cereal seeds. Six major types are dent, flint, flour, sweet, pop and pod corns. Used whole or processed into a multitude of products including sweeteners, flours, and oils.

polenta

Cooked corn. Comes either dry or packaged ready to use.

flaxseed and flaxseed meal

Seed of ancient medicinal herb, with a nutty flavor. Used whole, toasted or sprouted; ground into meal; or pressed into oil. High in fiber.

gluten-free baking powder

Made from baking soda and creme of tartar and essential to a completely gluten-free baked good. Gluten-free baking powder can be bought at your local grocery store.

xanthan gum

Used as a stabilizer, emulsifier, thickener, and holds baked products together that are gluten-free. It is also used as a thickener in fruit juices, as well as in the formation of various low-calorie foods. It is gluten-free, should be used with other gluten-free flours, and made from vegetable cellulose.

maca and roasted maca

A nourishing yellow colored root vegetable from the Andes mountains of Peru, it is ground into a powder and can be used as a partial flour substitute in any recipe calling for gluten-free flour. Maca has a malt taste and blends well with carob and raw cacao powder to make a chocolate malt flavor. The benefits of maca include hormonal health, increased libido, and athletic performance. Maca also comes roasted and tastes like coffee and has a dark brown color.

hemp protein powder

Comes organic and is made with hemp seeds. Hemp contains protein, fiber, and Omega 3, 6, 9 fats. It is a great alternative to whey protein powder. Hemp Protein Powder can supply any diet with a vegetarian source of essential fatty acids, antioxidants, vitamins, minerals, fiber, chlorophyll and a complete, balanced gluten-free source of the essential amino acids.

rice protein powder

Gluten-free and an alternative to soy, this protein powder is made from ground brown rice. Rice protein is derived by carefully isolating the protein from brown rice. It is a complete protein containing all essential and nonessential amino acids. Rice protein is hypoallergenic, which makes it suitable for everyone.

whey protein powder

Whey protein is made from milk and is a common protein supplement. It contains nonessential and essential amino acids, as well as branch chain amino acids (BCAA). Amino acids are the building blocks of protein. The body does not make essential amino acids, therefore they must be obtained through diet. Nonessential amino acids can be synthesized by the body. Whey protein is not appropriate for those who are lactose intolerant.

lactose-free whey protein powder

The same as whey protein powder but the lactose is removed and this makes it easier for those to digest who have allergies to milk products. Lactose-free whey protein powder is used in many Sweet Truth recipes and can be found at your local health food store.

wheat-free whole grains

quinoa

Known as the Mother Grain from South America, quinoa is a staple in my kitchen. Is it in yours? Maybe not yet, but it will be soon. My personal favorite brand is Ancient Harvest: organic flakes, flour and grain. The grains come in a colorful selection of red or white. The red has a nutty taste and can be mixed with the white to make an eye-opening and appealing dish.

Replace pasta and bread with quinoa and you will lose weight. Another amazing benefit to using quinoa instead of wheat is reduction of inflammation throughout the body, thereby reducing pain. Because it is gluten-free, digestion of this wonder grain is easy. It is also not addictive like wheat can be. High in protein, quinoa -- like buckwheat -- contains eight essential amino acids.

This is great news for anyone who would like to help along their digestion by eliminating animal protein at their evening meal and replacing it with quinoa, vegetables, and toasted sesame oil, for example. Combine this versatile grain with spices like turmeric and cumin for more increased digestion, absorption and - yes, elimination. Quinoa is truly a wonder food for beauty and WEIGHT LOSS!

Quinoa can be boiled, baked, braised, fried. Its texture can be soft-heavy-moist or fluffy-light-dry. If you are new to this grain, start off with half basmati rice and half quinoa. Grains cook in 15 minutes. Use water, organic veggie broth, spices, fruit juices, or almond milk to make savory and sweet dishes using quinoa. Deepen color with beet or carrot juice for the creative cook in you.

quinoa flakes

Partially cooked and flaked quinoa. Makes a great breakfast cereal that cooks up in 90 seconds. Flakes can also be added to muffins and pancakes as a gluten-free alternative. Quinoa flakes and grains are used every day in my pantry.

buckwheat groats

Buckwheat is an amazing whole food. It comes in groats, or a small triangular seed. I buy my buckwheat in bulk and use it in my pancakes, muffins, cereals, breakfast breads, and candy. Like quinoa, it is high in protein and contains eight essential amino acids (eight proteins that the body cannot manufacture). Great news for vegetarians, but the best part about buckwheat is the fiber.

To me, as a so-called grain, nothing can compare. I say so-called because it is not a grain but, botanically speaking, a fruit and cousin to the rhubarb plant. Its digestibility and elimination properties without irritation to the digestive system are superior to any bran or oat product I've tried. For people who struggle with wheat allergies or gluten-intolerance, buckwheat is ideal. It has plenty of protein, B vitamins, and is rich in phosphorus, potassium, iron, and calcium. For me it aids in keeping my metabolism steady with no empty carb calories. This is a key factor in creating a steady blood sugar balance and aids in easy weight loss. Other known health benefits of buckwheat are that it may lower blood glucose, cholesterol, prevent fat accumulation, and promote safe and regular bowel movements. This information saved my life.

It also contains Rutin, vitamin P, and Choline. Rutin is a powerful bioflavonoid and is found in great quantities in buckwheat. Oddly, it is not found in other grains (rice, wheat, etc.) or even in beans! Rutin strengthens capillaries and aids against hardening of the arteries and high blood pressure. Vitamin P also increases capillary strength, but also functions to help absorb Vitamin C. And Choline plays an important role in metabolism. It lowers blood pressure and hinders the deposit of fat in the liver. Good for people who drink a lot of sugar. Namely, beer!

kashi or toasted buckwheat

When the triangular groat seed is roasted, it is called Kasha or kashi which is a Russian staple dish. Toasted buckwheat groats have a nutty flavor.

brown rice

The whole grain of rice, from which the germ and outer layers containing the bran have not been removed; unpolished rice.

millet

A highly digestible small white grain that is non-glutenous like quinoa and buckwheat.

sweet truth top vegetables root and sea

yams

Yams are my number one pick for sweet tooth satisfaction and keeping my body weigh in balance

Yams are in my pancakes, breakfast breads, and dehydrator protein cookies. Yams complex carbohydrates and fiber deliver sweet tasting carbs gradually, slowing the rate at which their complex sugars are released and absorbed into the bloodstream. This is important in keeping the blood sugar level even. The fiber is filling and important for good digestion.

As far as weight loss, they are the ultimate root vegetable for bodybuilders and waist trimmers because yams are a good source of manganese, a trace mineral that helps with carbohydrate metabolism and is a vital player in a number of enzymatic processes that are important in energy production, antioxidant defenses, and boosting the immune system.

sea vegetables

Seaweed, better known to affluent vegetarian Americans as "sea vegetables" -- is the ultimate elixir for balancing the body, especially if taken on a daily basis. In macrobiotic cooking they are used to strengthen the blood, heart and circulatory system, as well as support the health of the kidneys, urinary system,, and reproductive organs.

My favorites that are always stocked in my pantry are nori, walkame, arame, hijiki, kombu, agar agar, and kuzu, (See next page for description). Getting your greens doesn't always have to mean eating bitter kale. Yes, you can take a pro-greens drink (which I encourage), but to me, it's not the same as eating these delicate, nutrient-dense miracle foods of the ocean mother. In my recipes like Mermaid Salad, I use hijiki for strong hair and arame to heal the hormonal synergy of the female system. Both of these sea vegetables are packed with calcium, iron, iodine, and selenium which increases blood circulation and heart functions; therefore, your 'horse power' will be revved up and ready to go! It serves well as a salty side dish or with quinoa, turmeric,sea salt, and toasted sesame oil for diner.

The last thing I want to talk about is seaweed, yet it's the most important to healing sugar addiction. Even though it is grown in oceans, lakes and rivers from Japan to the New England coast of Maine and even in Ireland, you can find it at any health foods store, even order online. If you want to be more healthy, eat seaweed, but if you want to heal your hair and skin, definitely eat seaweed everyday. You can use them in side dishes, soups, salads, cooked with grains, beans or vegetables. They are high in iodine and iron. Iron content in a 3.5 oz serving of sea weed is: arame 12 mg, wakame 13 mg, kombu 15 mg, hijiki 29 mg, dulse 6 mg, nori 23 mg. For comparison, liver has only 8 mg. I'd rather eat sea vegetables than liver.

Sea weed is beneficial to eat because, like the deep ocean, our blood has the same slightly salty composition where primordial life originated. The complex carbs and fiber in sea vegetables are softer than land plants and more digestible. So it's good to eat a balance of land veggies and sea veggies. The reason the sea veggies are softer is because they sway in the water. Supposedly, in a macrobiotic diet, these underwater plants can enhance the flexibility of the mind and spirit.

Sea veggies strengthen the blood, the heart, and the circulatory system. They are also excellent for the kidneys, urinary tract and reproductive system. They give elasticity to veins, arteries, and organ tissues contributing to the flexibility of the bodies many interrelated systems. Restorative and preventive, arame helps to balance female system. Hijiki and walkame strengthen the intestines and produce beautiful shiny strong hair and purifies the blood. Kombu and nori help to reduce high blood pressure and reduce cholesterol levels. They all help with fat metabolism. Especially, nori, wakame, hijiki and kombu.

The people with the highest longevity on the planet live on Oki Island in Japan. Among other Japanese, the Okinawans eat the highest volumes of sea vegetables. I have found that since beginning to eat sea weed, my hair has grown back and fall out is 75% better. I have been consistently losing weight without trying, the result of excluding sugar and eating lots of sea veggies.

sweet truth sea vegetables

arame

Arame has a mild flavor and is dried and cut into thin strands. It can be added to soups, salads, or served as a vegetable side dish. Arame is known to be beneficial for women's health.

kombu

Kombu can be used for soup stock, or added to the bottom of a pot of rice or vegetables to help them keep from sticking, or added to a pot of beans to help reduce the gas from the beans. Kombu has been used to help high blood pressure.

wakame

Wakame is a popular and well known sea vegetable found in the miso soup that you are served at sushi restaurants. It is a good source of protein, iron, calcium, sodium and other minerals and vitamins and aids fat metabolism.

agar-agar

Even though it appears clear, this red algae is served as a versatile, tasty gel that will set at room temperature, but sets best in the refrigerator especially when cooked fruit has been added to make a Japanese dessert called kanten. It is also great for digestion and is rich in iodine and trace elements.

nori

Unlike other sea vegetables that are collected wild, Japanese nori is cultivated and is used as the wrapping for sushi. It can also be cut into squares and eaten as a snack. It is high in vitamin A and protein.

hijiki

Found primarily in the Far East, contains the most calcium of any of the sea vegetables, 1400mg/100gr dry weight (compared to milk with 100mg/100gr). I like the small type of hijiki best for salads. I use hijiki to strengthen the intestines, the hair, and purify and strengthen the blood.

kuzu

a Japanese root starch that is non-glutenous and used to make puddings and thicken sauces and soups.

dulse

A red algae that is ground into a powder and can be used as a salt or sodium replacement. Good in soups and stews.

other green power foods

green powders

Found in health food stores, green powders are made of green vegetables like spinach, green grasses like wheat grass, sea vegetables like dulse, plus spirulina and chorella. Add to smoothies.

spirulina

A blue green algae that is rich in proteins, vitamins, minerals, and anti-oxidants. It is highly digestible and contains amino acids, RNA and DNA. It helps to lower cholesterol and enhance mineral absorption.

chorella

A green algae that contains high levels of chlorophyll, as well as protein, vitamins, and amino acids that help to boost the immune system and detoxify the body. Add chorella and spirulina to raw treats and desserts.

setting up your dairy-free pantry

I like using dairy-free products as much as possible for better digestion. Most of the recipes in this cookbook use dairy-free ingredients, but not all do, and you are always free to substitute. For example, you may replace butter with vegetable butter, and shortening with vegetable shortening. Yogurt may be switched out for unflavored soy yogurt, unsweetened soy milk or unsweetened almond milk.

Setting up your dairy-free pantry is easy. And if you are worried about small amounts of gluten hidden in the malted barley used to make rice syrup which is the main sweetener used sweeten most milk alternatives like unsweetened almond milk, rice milk, soy milk, hazel nut milk, and oat milk. I suggest to use unsweetened almond milk and unsweetened soy milk which can be found in 32 oz containers. To sweeten, just add 1 tablespoon of agave and 2 droppers of Liquid Stevia Vanilla Creme for a sweetened gluten-free milk alternative.

Recipe Note: To make your own instant gluten-free sweetened nut milk, place 2 cups raw, unsalted organic cashews in Vita Mix, and cover with water to the top of the nuts. Add 1 cup ice and puree. Add 2 tablespoons light agave and 2 droppers of Liquid Stevia Vanilla Creme and blend until smooth. The same recipe can be duplicated with hemp seeds. For both cashews and hemp, no overnight soaking is needed.

To make almond milk, soak 2 cups of raw, unsalted organic almonds in 3 cups of water over night. Drain and rinse nuts and add to Vita Mix. Cover almonds with water to the top of the nuts. Add 1 cup of ice and puree. Add 2 tablespoons light agave and 2 droppers Liquid Stevia Vanilla Creme and blend until smooth. Keeps for several days in the refrigerator.

almond milk and unsweetened almond milk

If it is store-bought, it's usually made from almonds and sweetened with brown rice syrup that contains malted barley which is glutenous. Almond milk also comes unsweetened and is made by Blue Diamond. Or it's easy make your own gluten-free low glycemic almond milk, cashew milk, or hemp seed milk (see immediately above).

rice milk

Made from rice and sweetened with brown rice syrup or corn syrup.

soy milk and unsweetened soy milk

Made from soybeans and sweetened with brown rice syrup or corn syrup. Best choice for a gluten-free, dairy-free milk alternative made from soybeans. Unsweetened soy usually has 9 grams of fat per serving, but because it is not sweetened, I really like the effect on my body -- I tend to drink a lot less of it compared to a sweetened milk alternative.

unsweetened low fat coconut milk

Made from coconut meat.

vegetable butter

Comes organic and is made from soybeans, palm fruit, canola, and olive oils and contains saturated and unsaturated fats.

vegetable shortening

Comes organic and is made from palm oil, a saturated fat.

dairy and dairy-free substitutes

A few recipes in The Sweet Truth cookbook are made with real dairy, like heavy cream and agave for a whipped dessert topping, but you may use a cashew cream in its place. Remember, there are always substitutes. In the following section, I have given you healthy alternatives to the dairy I use in the recipe or dairy-free substitutes primarily using unsweetened soy as to avoid the hidden gluten in malted corn and barley used to sweeten dairy-free products like almond milk and rice milk.

Although I avoid the gluten found in grains like wheat and barley at all costs, I sometimes use almond milk and rice milk which contain small amounts of gluten found in brown rice syrup when I don't have time to make my own dairy-free milk or don't have an unsweetened almond milk on hand. If you want to be absolutely gluten-free, make your own nut or seed milk and use cup for cup in any recipe.

cow's milk or powdered non-fat milk

May be substituted with any milk alternative like almond or unsweetened soy. For powdered non-fat dry milk (like in the recipe for my Toddler Teething Biscuits), substitute 1/2 cup non-fat dry milk with 1/4 cup pure rice protein powder and 1/4 cup milk alternative.

yogurt
May be substituted with unflavored soy yogurt or unsweetened soy milk.

sour cream
May be substituted with Greek style yogurt for a healthy dairy substitute or soy yogurt for a dairy-free substitute or unsweetened soy milk.

heavy cream
Used for whipped topping on desserts and sweetened with light agave

recipe note for dairy-free whipped cream:
To make a dairy-free whipped cream, take 1 cup raw, unsalted macadamia nuts, 1 cup raw, unsalted cashews, 1/2 cup, unsweetened almond milk, 2 tablespoons light agave, 2 droppers Liquid Stevia Vanilla Creme, and place in Vita Mix. Blend until smooth. Serve immediately.

low-fat butter milk
May be substituted with 1 cup unsweetened soy and 1/2 teaspoon lemon juice for each cup of low-fat butter milk.

sweet truth good oils

The facts about bad fats are this: Saturated fats raise total blood cholesterol as well as LDL cholesterol (the bad cholesterol). Trans fats raise LDL cholesterol (the bad cholesterol) and lower HDL cholesterol (the good cholesterol). Why then do I use Extra Virgin Coconut Oil, a saturated fat? I use it because it is a short chain saturated fat that has been found to metabolize faster than long chain saturated fats and has been found to help stimulate metabolism.

The facts about good fats are these: Monounsaturated fats lower total cholesterol and LDL cholesterol (the bad cholesterol) and increase the HDL cholesterol (the good cholesterol). Polyunsaturated fats also lower total cholesterol and LDL cholesterol. Omega 3 fatty acids belong to this group such as **Flax Seed Oil, Extra Virgin Olive Oil, and Hemp Seed Oil. Toasted sesame oil** is another beneficial mono-saturated fat that I use in dressings and with grains.

other sweet staples

nut and seed butters

Organic raw, non-salted tahini, almond butter, cashew butter, black tahini, peanut butter, macadamia nut butter, and sunflower butter. I use these in moderation, no more than 2 teaspoons per serving.

let's get shopping and make a list

Starting a list is easy and is my key to success. I only use three sugar alternatives, agave, stevia, and zeratol and gluten-free flour and xanthan gum take care of most recipes calling for wheat flour. Everything else is a whole food and can be found at your local market.

Most of the ingredients you already have in your pantry. The best thing you can do is make a top twelve list of the new and exciting items. They may sound exotic, but soon will become second nature staples in your Sweet Truth pantry. Start with one recipe: write down all the ingredients you don't have or have no idea where to find. If you live near a health food store, make a field trip and if they don't carry it, ask them to special order, or purchase the items on-line. (See on-line ordering info).

The following top twelve list along with you regular pantry ingredients makes my famous 90 second gourmet truffle called FUDGE IT, as well as FOUR YAM MASH, MERMAID SALAD, PUMPKIN PANCAKES, NO GUILT BROWNIES, and SMART COOKIES/CAROB CHIP. Plus lots more.

On the following page, these top twelve Sweet Truth sugar-free/wheat-free pantry items are my "can't live without" food items and just a suggestion to get started. You can pick your own recipe and make a top twelve list to suit you!

kelly's top 12

- light agave nectar
- Liquid Stevia Vanilla Creme
- roasted carob powder
- unsweetened carob chips
- buckwheat groats
- raw organic tahini no salt added
- almond or unsweetened soy milk
- xanthan gum
- gluten-free flour
- quinoa grains
- nori and sea vegetables
- yams

kelly's shopping list for on-line ordering

AGAVE NECTAR and VITAMIX
www.kellykeough.com

STEVIA Plus Powder, STEVIA LIQUID DROPS
www.sweetleaf.com

ZERATOL/SWERVE
www.pcflabs.com

QUINOA FLAKES, QUINOA GRAINS, QUINOA FLOUR
www.ancientharvest.com

BUCKWHEAT GROATS, BUCKWHEAT FLOUR
www.arrowheadmills.com

HIMALAYAN GOJI BERRY JUICE
www.kellykeough.com

EXTRA VIRGIN COCONUT OIL
www.nutiva.com

HEMP SEEDS. HEMP OIL. HEMP BUTTER
www.nutiva.com
www.manitoba.com

ALMOND BUTTER, ORGANIC RAW TAHINI, CASHEW BUTTER, ETC.
www.maranantha.com

MACA & ROASTED MACA
www.healthywiseorganics.com

XANTHAN GUM, GLUTEN-FREE FLOURS & BAKING POWDER
www.bobredmills.com

YACON SLICES & POWDER
www.macaweb.com

STRAWBERRY POWDER
Wilderness Family Naturals at 866-936-6457.

GOJI BERRYS, RAW CACAO NIBS
www.naturesfirstlaw.com

sugar-free baking techniques and tips

Sugar turns liquid in the baking or heating process so one of the best replacements for sugar in baking and cooking is agave. Like sugar, agave gives volume, moistness, sweetness, browning and caramelization to the recipe. Agave is my number one choice also because the taste is so delicious -- like maple syrup of honey, and because it is diabetic-safe. That means it has a low GI and won't spike the blood sugar like sugar, honey, maple syrup, Splenda, sugar-alcohols like xylitol, and the fake sugars like Sweet N' Low.

Pick a recipe with a best friend or baking buddy, pitch in for ingredients, and divide them in half to get an inexpensive jump start to your sugar-free pantry. Most recipes use agave and stevia which are affordable, inexpensive, and good investment in your health.

Replacing sugar in a recipe is about still wanting to eat sweets but not having to endure the ill effects of processed white sugar. My intention is to not only make a dessert or dish that is sugar-free, but also cuts out unnecessary carbs and calories. Agave and yacon have low GI's and stevia and zeratol have zero GI's and no calories.

Use a combination of sugar-free alternatives because the blending of the flavors creates the best sweet taste that will satisfy people who still have white sugar and white flour taste buds (especially kids who are exposed to that food in their daily life outside the home).

Recipes that call for 1 1/2 cups of sugar can be replaced with 1/2 cup of agave (light or dark), plus 2 teaspoons stevia plus powder, 2 droppers of a liquid stevia, and 1/2 cup yacon or zeratol. Using this combination will extend the value of your sugar-free pantry, especially because zeratol has a high price point. Replacement volume does not match, but the other liquids or fruit in the recipe will make up for the missing sugar volume. Also, if you want a sweeter tasting product, increase agave by two tablespoons in a given recipe.

Eating is also a technique. So, here's a tip. A Sweet Truth dessert recipe is still a dessert. If you are making cookies, have two. If it is anything else, all you need is one.

wheat/gluten-free baking techniques and tips

Wheat has gluten, a gluey protein chain that gives baked goods their form, rise, and hold-it-togetherness. Baking wheat-free and gluten-free means there are none of these sticky helper properties. To replace the gluten, use about 1 teaspoon of xanthan gum with a combination of gluten-free flours. My favorite gluten-free flour is an all-purpose flour that already combines garbanzo, garfava, tapioca, and potato starch for you. This flour is great for cookies, muffins, and scones.

Silicon bake ware is best for sticky gluten-free dough and batters because it doesn't have to be oiled and dusted. If you are using baby Bundt silicon trays, you may want to spray, but no dusting is needed.

Dough and batter are best dealt with a long, flat spatula that has been spray oiled.

Glass baking dishes are good for brownies if you don't have silicon, but any bake ware will do if you properly prepare it with a light coat of spray oil and a dusting of gluten-free flour.

Spray oil on hands for touching sticky gluten-free dough and batter. You may also spray oil the back of a flat dry measuring cup to even out tart dough or to flatten rounded cookies.

White rice flour is the absolute best for dusting spray oiled bake ware and when rolling out dough between two sheets of wax paper. Its grainy, non-stick texture acts as an excellent barrier between the dough or batter and your hands or bake ware.

Foil tents used over pies, coffee cakes, breads, and scones -- basically all baked goods -- will save your masterpieces and ensure they will turn golden and not burn.

Oven thermometers are key in monitoring your baking or roasting temperatures. Gluten free flours tend to brown quickly and an overheated oven will burn your dough, batter, or crust.

kitchen equipment, cookware, and bake ware

Vita Mix blender
11 cup food processor
3 cup mini-food processor
5 tray Excaliber dehydrator with Teflex sheets & mesh sheets
Stand up mixer with wire and paddle attachment
small, medium, large mixing bowls
medium sauce pan, large skillet, 8 quart soup pan
9 inch pie glass pie plate
8x8 glass baking dish
9x12 glass baking dish
baking sheets
roasting pan
rolling pin
liquid and dry measuring cups
measuring spoons
one oz shot glass
sturdy sifter
Kitchen Aid long spatula
Teflon coated frying pan
waffle iron
pancake griddle
small wire strainer
large colander
large wire strainer
vegetable peeler
bamboo mat
heavy duty coffee grinder
ice cream maker
large cup cake tins
mini cup cake tins
two, 9 inch cake tins
12 cup Bundt cake pan
tube cake pan
great set of knives
cutting boards
fruit and vegetable juicer
martini shaker

if you crave that	eat this
French Fries	**Sunset Strips**
Fudge	**Fudge It Ball Truffles**
Cake	**Miami Beach Bikini Cake**
Bran Muffins	**Courageous Carrot Cake Muffins**
Frozen Yogurt	**Ice Cream Any Day**
Jelly or Jam	**Blueberry Babe**
Peanut Butter Cookies	**Peanut Butter Paws**
Sugar, Honey, Maple Syrup, Rice Syrup	**Stevia, Agave Nectar, Swerve**
Croutons	**Polenta Pyramids**
Apple Pie	**Four Apple Dessert**
Bagel	**Wholly Cinnamon Bagel**
Scones	**Carob Chip Scone**
Cereal	**KooKoo Cocoa Cereal**
Bread	**The Other White Loaf**
Red Wine	**Tooty Fruity Sangria**
Chocolate Pudding	**Love Dove Carob Pudding**
Chocolate Mousse	**Baby Moose Mud**
Chocolate Chip Cookies	**Cleavage Chip Cookies**
Rice Pilaf	**Mermaid Salad**
Pumpkin Pie	**Kelly's Pumpkin Pie**
Sweet Muffins	**Magic Muffins w/Great Ganache**
Fudge Brownies	**NO Guilt Brownies**
Almond Joy	**Love Dove Cupid's Candy**
California Sushi Rolls	**Kelly's Cali Rolls**
Thai Food	**Cool Chick Coconut Curry**

menus

The Sweet Truth sugar-free/wheat-free food practice takes into account the different stages of weaning off sugar and flour. The following lists are partial menu suggestions and a guideline of what I did to get off sugar and keep my food practice consistent. Add extra vegetables, raw salads, and protein where you want.

Just starting, I fed my sugar craving for the first six weeks and ate one serving of two substantial sugar-free low glycemic desserts a day. It may take three months, but the important thing to remember is to not deprive the body and taste buds, but instead satisfy without overeating and spiking the blood sugar.

When I stopped craving white sugar and was satisfied knowing I wasn't going to die without sugar, I switched the intensity of my dessert recipes and lightened up on my meals: not every day, but my body told me when to cut back while still satisfying my sweet tooth physically and emotionally without gaining weight.

Then after months of consistently cooking sweet dishes from breakfast to dinner and two planned snacks, my body still wants sweets, but a different variety of desserts, snacks, and dishes that include more fruit and sea vegetables. During holidays and special occasions, I indulge, but only with my own decadent recipes like Voluptuous Volcano Cake.

(Week one - six) Just starting to get off sugar...

BREAKFAST

Blueberry Cornbread Muffins
Organic green tea.

10:00 SNACK

Fudge It

LUNCH

Sweet Lentil Stew
You Can't Beet That Puree.

3:00 SNACK

No Guilt Brownie

DINNER

Gourmet Garden Turkey Burgers
quinoa
Four Apple Dessert

(Weeks seven - twelve) Need something a little extra...

BREAKFAST

Queen Quinoa

10:00 SNACK

Blueberry Breakfast Bread

LUNCH

Cool Chick Coconut Curry

Quinoa

Arugula salad with toasted sesame oil and spices.

3:00 SNACK

Home Made Hummus with Lemon Lotus Chips

DINNER

Sunset Strips

Beets and Leeks Lampoon

(Weeks thirteen and beyond) Feeling good today...

BREAKFAST

Star Buckwheat Pancakes

Atta Girl Apricot

Organic green tea.

10:00 SNACK

Think Pink Think Thin

LUNCH

Salmon

Mermaid Salad

Fennel and Mushroom Rush.

3:00 SNACK

Apple Flaxx Jax Crackers w/almond butter

DINNER

Love It Lentil Loaf

Salad w/sunflower sprouts and Sunflower Dressing.

last looks...

Planning, preparing, and enjoying foods like these from THE SWEET TRUTH list, you'll find an abundance of sweetness. And isn't that what life is all about? Sweet pleasure? The reason that you'll be able to have your sweets and eat them too, without feeling a compulsion to overeat, is because there is no refined white sugar or wheat flour to trigger a biochemical reaction of addiction in the brain chemistry, nor will eating THE SWEET TRUTH recipes that follow elicit feelings of guilt and other negative connotations most women associate with carbs and desserts thanks to the diet crazes of popular culture.

Practicing no sugar/no flour with THE SWEET TRUTH is easy with the Three "P's" and the Top Twelve Sweet Truth Ingredients. And if time is an issue, you know the drill, hire someone. At least once a week, make a grain, a dessert, a sweet veggie, a pulse (beans or lentils), and a fruit dish.

THE SWEET TRUTH food practice is aimed at putting the sweet back into life and, therefore, the pleasure. When is the last time you had a pleasurable meal?

Again and again, here's to your culinary destiny...

cookies and brownies

no guilt brownies

hemp brownies

carob protein dehydrator cookies

oatmeal wheels

smart cookie chocolate chip

smart cookie peanut butter paws

cleavage chip cookies on a stick

cry babies

coconut smacky mackys

goddess guccidotti

cut out sugar cookies

sicily biscotti

no guilt brownies

A protein packed, carob brownie. A mini-meal you can eat for breakfast or a 3 o'clock snack.

2 Omega 3 organic eggs
1/4 cup plus 2 tablespoons agave
1 1/2 tablespoons organic vanilla
3/4 cup coconut date rolls, or Medjool dates
1/2 cup unsweetened almond milk
15 oz can organic black beans, drained
1/2 cup organic raw tahini (no salt added)
6 packets or 3 teaspoons Stevia Plus Powder
2 teaspoons cinnamon
3/4 cup carob powder
1/2 cup buckwheat flour
1 teaspoon baking powder
1 teaspoon baking soda
1 teaspoon xanthan gum
3/4 cup unsweetened carob chips
1/2 cup chopped Brazil nuts

Preheat oven to 350 degrees. Add to food processor, eggs, agave, and vanilla. Puree until mixed. Add dates and almond milk and puree until well blended. Add black beans, tahini, Stevia, and cinnamon. Pulse until well blended. Add in carob powder and pulse slowly until mixed. Now it starts to look like a brownie mix.

In separate small bowl blend well, buckwheat flour, baking powder, baking soda, and xanthan gum. Slowly add prepared flour mixture into food processor. Pulse until just blended. Remember, the brownie mixture will appear very thick. Add in chips and pulse a few times.

Transfer the mixture to an 8x8 pan that has been sprayed with cooking spray and lightly floured with buckwheat flour. Use a bit of spray oil on your spatula for easy spreading. Spread brownie mixture evenly and sprinkle chopped Brazil nuts on top of brownie mixture.

Bake at 350 degrees for 45-50 minutes.

Yield: 16 brownies.

hemp brownies

A rich brownie with the many benefits of hemp's Omega 3, 6, and 9.

1/2 cup carob powder
1/4 cup unsweetened Valrhona cocoa powder
1/2 cup brown rice flour
3 tablespoons maca powder
6 packets or 3 teaspoons Stevia Plus powder
2 droppers Liquid Stevia Dark Chocolate
1 1/2 tablespoons organic vanilla
2 Omega 3 eggs
2 tablespoons melted extra virgin coconut oil
1/2 cup dates
1 can 15 oz organic Navy beans
1/2 cup almond milk
1/2 cup organic hemp butter
1/4 cup plus an extra 2 tablespoons agave for topping
1 teaspoon baking powder
1 teaspoon xanthan gum
1/2 cup organic hemp seeds plus extra for topping

Preheat oven to 350 degrees. It's best to use a stand up mixer or do everything by hand because the brownie batter is meant to be thick. Beat eggs, agave, melted coconut oil, and vanilla in medium bowl. Next, in food processor, puree dates and almond milk, then add beans (drained), hemp butter, Stevia, cinnamon and puree again. Combine this batter to eggs mixture in stand up mixer.

Slowly add in carob powder, followed by unsweetened cocoa, and maca. Now it starts to look like a brownie mix. In separate bowl, blend, flour, baking powder, and xanthan gum. Slowly add prepared dry mixture to wet mixture and blend. Remember, the brownie mixture will feel very thick. Fold 1/2 cup hemp seeds. Spoon mixture into an 8x8 pan that has been dusted with cooking spray and lightly floured with brown rice flour.

Sprinkle extra hemp seeds on top and then drizzle the extra 2 tablespoons agave over seeds in a crisscross pattern. Bake at 350 degrees for 45 minutes or until a knife test comes out clean from the middle of the pan.

Yield: 16 brownies.

carob protein dehydrator cookies

A high protein, lo carb cookie made with protein powder, buckwheat groats, and agave.

1 cup soaked and sprouted buckwheat groats
1/2 cup cooked yam with skin
1/3 cup organic raw no salt tahini
3 droppers Liquid Stevia Vanilla Creme
1/2 cup rice or lactose-free whey protein powder
3 tablespoons dark agave
1/2 cup almond milk
2 teaspoons cinnamon
3 rounded tablespoons roasted carob
1 rounded tablespoons cocoa powder
1 tablespoon vanilla
2 tablespoons ground raw cacao nibs and Goji berries

To soak and sprout buckwheat: In a small covered container, soak 3/4 cup dry buckwheat groats in 2 cups filtered water overnight in your refrigerator. In the morning, drain in big colander. You may use buckwheat soaked or continue to sprout. To sprout -- use spatula to press the buckwheat groats to the sides of the colander so there is an even amount around the colander. Place on top of a plate to catch water from dripping out and cover with plastic wrap. Cut holes in plastic wrap with knife and set to sprout out of the sun in a cool dry place. Within 24-36 hours, the buckwheat will sprout baby tails. That's when you know it's done. Place in a container and refrigerate until use. You will have over one cup of sprouted buckwheat so measure before you start the recipe.

Set dehydrator at 105 degrees. In food processor, puree all the ingredients until smooth. Spoon a rounded tablespoon each of the mixture onto dehydrator sheets. Place 16 spoonfuls to a sheet.

With back of spoon in a circular motion, flatten each of the cookies into a 1/4 inch high round shape. Sprinkle each cookie with coconut. Dehydrate for 16-20 hours depending on how chewy or crunchy you like your cookies. Store in an air tight container for two weeks,

Yield: 36 cookies.

oatmeal wheels

A chewy, spiced apple cookie with raisins and macadamia nuts.

1 cup slow cook oats plus another 1/2 cup oats set aside
3/4 cup coconut date rolls
1/2 cup spiced apple cider
2 tablespoons dark agave
2 droppers Liquid Stevia Vanilla Creme
2 teaspoons cinnamon
1/2 cup unsweetened coconut
1 Fuji apple, sliced
1/4 cup raisins
1/4 cup coarsely chopped raw macadamia nuts

In food processor, use pulse action to mix 1 cup oats, date rolls, apple cider, agave, Liquid Stevia, cinnamon, coconut, and sliced apple. Once batter is mixed, puree and blend until batter is smooth.

Remove batter from processor and put into a medium mixing bowl. Stir in raisins, nuts, and extra oats. Form into 1/2 inch high flat wheel shapes on a Teflex dehydrator baking sheet. Dehydrate at 105 degrees for 16–20 hours. Half way through the dehydration process, use a spray oiled spatula and flip cookies over. Continue to dehydrate. Keep in an air tight container for up to two weeks.

Note: This recipe uses a dehydrator and the cookies are not baked. If you don't have a dehydrator, place cookies on a parchment lined baking sheet and bake at 200 degrees for one hour, turn cookies over and bake another 30 minutes.

Gluten-free substitute: Oats can contain gluten because sometimes they are cross-contaminated with wheat. You may also use 1 cup of soaked buckwheat groats by measuring 3/4 cup dry hulled buckwheat groats and soaking in 2 cups water overnight. Also use an extra 1/2 cup dry like the recipe calls for.

Yield: 24 cookies.

smart cookie/chocolate chip

A cookie made with an energy elixir and grain sweetened chips.

1 tablespoon ground golden organic flax seed
1 tablespoon soy lecithin
1/4 cup organic green grapes
3/4 cup organic vegetable spread, or butter
2 tablespoons extra virgin coconut oil
1/2 cup light agave
1 Omega 3 organic egg
2 tablespoons vanilla
3 droppers Liquid Stevia Vanilla Creme
1/4 cup unsweetened coconut
1 3/4 cups gluten-free flour
1 teaspoon baking soda
1 teaspoon xanthan gum
3/4 cup grain sweet chocolate chips or unsweetened carob chips

Preheat oven to 350 degrees. To make energy elixir, blend in mini-food processor 1 tablespoon ground golden flax, 1 tablespoon lecithin, and 1/4 cup green grapes. Set aside. In stand up mixer with paddle attachment, cream 3/4 cup vegetable spread (or butter), 2 tablespoons extra virgin organic coconut oil, 1/2 cup agave, one Omega 3 organic egg, and 2 tablespoons vanilla. Then cream in the prepared energy elixir. Next, add 3 droppers Vanilla Stevia Liquid and 1/4 cup unsweetened fine coconut and blend.

In small bowl, sift together 1 3/4 cup gluten-free flour, 1 teaspoon baking soda, and 1 teaspoon xanthan gum. Add prepared dry ingredients slowly to wet batter and blend.

Consistency should be thick just like a cookie batter. Stir in 3/4 cup grain sweetened chocolate chips or use unsweetened carob chips for a gluten-free cookie. Form into 2 inch domes and place each cookie a parchment lined un-greased cookie sheet. Freeze formed uncooked cookies for at least 30 minutes. Bake for 11-12 minutes. Cool on wire rack.

Note: To grind flax seeds, place in a coffee grinder until finely ground.

Yield: 24 small cookies.

smart cookie/peanut butter paws

A cookie made with an energy elixir and organic peanut butter.

1 tablespoon ground golden flax seed
1 tablespoon soy lecithin
1/4 cup organic Fuji apple, finely chopped
3/4 cup vegetable spread, or butter
1 cup organic peanut butter
1/2 cup light agave
1 Omega 3 organic egg
2 tablespoons vanilla
2 packets or 4 teaspoons Stevia Plus Powder
1 cup quinoa flour
1 cup gluten-free baking flour
1 teaspoon baking soda
1 teaspoon xanthan gum
1/2 cup raw organic peanuts (optional)

Preheat oven to 350 degrees. Make Energy Elixir by blending in mini-food processor 1 tablespoon ground golden flax, 1 tablespoon soy lecithin, and 1/4 cup Fuji apple. Set aside.

In stand up mixing bowl with paddle attachment, cream 3/4 cup vegetable spread (or butter), 1 cup organic peanut butter, 1/2 cup agave, one Omega 3 organic egg, and 2 tablespoons vanilla. Then cream in the prepared Energy Elixir plus 4 teaspoons Stevia Plus Powder.

In small bowl, sift together 1 cup quinoa flour, 1 cup gluten-free baking powder, 1 teaspoon baking soda, and 1 teaspoon xanthan gum. Add prepared flour mixture slowly to batter and blend. Consistency should be thick just like a cookie batter. Stir in 1/2 cup chopped raw peanuts (optional).

Form into 2 inch domes and place each cookie on a parchment lined ungreased cookie sheet. Spray oil a fork and make crisscross marks in each cookie. Freeze formed uncooked cookies for at least 30 minutes. Bake for 11-12 minutes in 350 degree oven. Cool on a wire rack.

Note: To grind flax seeds, place in a coffee grinder until finely ground.

Yield: 24 small cookies.

cleavage chip cookies on a stick

A huge grain sweetened chocolate chip cookie on a stick.

1 cup pecan halves
2 cups plus 2 tablespoons gluten-free flour
2 teaspoons baking soda
2 teaspoons xanthan gum
3/4 teaspoon sea salt
1 cup vegetable butter
1/2 cup Swerve sugar substitute
1/2 cup dark agave
2 droppers Liquid Stevia Vanilla Creme
2 droppers Liquid Stevia Dark Chocolate
1 organic Omega 3 egg
1 organic Omega 3 egg yolk
2 tablespoons pure vanilla extract
3/4 cup of grain sweetened chocolate chip
1 1/2 cups unsweetened puffed brown rice, slightly crushed

Preheat oven to 350 degrees. In dry Teflon coated sauté pan, place pecans over a medium heat and toast nuts until oils are released about 8 minutes. Immediately transfer nuts to a bowl and set aside.

In a large mixing bowl, sift together gluten-free flour, baking soda, xanthan gum, and salt. Set aside. In medium saucepan, melt vegetable butter over medium heat. Turn off the heat under the butter. With wire whisk, add in Swerve and agave to butter mixture. Whisk until combined. Pour into large mixing bowl to cool slightly.

Into the melted butter mixture add, Liquid Stevias, egg, egg yolk, and vanilla. Add the prepared wet mixture to the large mixing bowl containing pre-sifted flour mixture and stir until just combined. Let dough cool completely at room temperature. When cookie dough is cooled mix in chocolate chips and nuts.

With a large spoon, scoop cookie dough into parchment lined baking tray about 2 inches apart. Spray oil hands so dough will not stick and form dough into balls. Spray oil the bottom of a small custard dish and flatten the cookie mounds slightly with the flat bottom and slide off the cookie. Do not pull the custard cup directly up or the dough with pull.

Place a Popsicle or cookie stick in the bottom a 1/3 of the way through at a 45-degree angle and place in the freezer for 30 minutes. Bake for 11-13 minutes. Remove from oven and cool for 2 minutes before transferring to wire rack.

Yield: 12 large cookies.

cry babies

My Gran's old fashioned, soft, caky cookie with a smiley face.

1 cup vegetable butter
1/2 cup vanilla rice protein powder
1 Omega 3 organic egg
1 cup unsweetened almond milk
1/2 cup dark agave
1 tablespoon vanilla
2 droppers Liquid Stevia Vanilla Creme
3 1/2 cups gluten-free flour
1/2 cup brown rice flour
3 teaspoons Stevia Plus Powder
2 teaspoons cinnamon
2 teaspoons baking soda
2 teaspoons xanthan gum
1/2 teaspoon salt
1/2 cup organic raisins

Preheat oven to 350 degrees. In stand up mixer with paddle attachment, cream butter and protein powder. Add in egg, milk, agave, vanilla and Liquid Stevia and beat until smooth.

In separate bowl, sift together gluten-free flour, baking powder, Stevia Plus Powder, cinnamon, baking soda, xanthan gum, and salt. Add prepared dry ingredients to wet ingredients. Batter is soft and fluffy and not dense like a regular cookie dough.

Spoon 12 large spoonfuls onto ungreased cookie sheet spaced evenly. Form into balls and flatten. Decorate face with raisins for eyes and smile or a frown. Freeze for 30 minutes. Bake for 12-15 minutes. Cool on wire rack.

Yield: 36 cookies.

coconut smacky mackys

A protein packed macaroon with vanilla protein powder and agave.

4 large organic egg whites
1/4 teaspoon cream of tartar
1 dropper Liquid Stevia Vanilla Creme
2 tablespoons light agave
1 teaspoon vanilla
1/2 teaspoon almond extract
2 cups unsweetened shredded coconut
1/4 cup vanilla rice or lactose-free whey protein powder
2 tablespoons tapioca starch
2 tablespoons almond meal
dash of salt

Preheat oven to 325 degrees. Spray baking sheet with non-stick spray and line with parchment paper.

In stand up mixer with wire attachment, whisk egg whites and cream of tartar until soft peaks are formed. Add in, Liquid Stevia, agave, vanilla extract, almond extract, and a dash of salt and beat until batter is shinny.

Carefully by hand, fold in coconut, protein powder, tapioca starch, and almond meal. Drop mixture by packed tablespoons onto prepared sheet. There should be 16 to a baking sheet. Bake 12-15 minutes. Cookies are done when slightly golden. Be careful not to over bake because cookies will harden. Taste is best when cooled an hour on wire rack.

Yield: 24 cookies.

goddess guccidotti

A Christmas fig cookie with sugar-free pink and green frosting.

DOUGH
1 cup organic vegetable shortening
1 1/2 cups yacon powder or Swerve sugar substitute
6 Omega 3 organic eggs
1 tablespoon vanilla extract
pinch salt
3 cups gluten-free flour
1 cup potato starch
3 teaspoons baking powder
1 teaspoon baking soda
3 teaspoons Stevia Plus Powder
2 teaspoons xanthan gum

FILLING
1 whole organic orange (with peel), coarsely chopped
1 small Fuji apple (with peel), sliced
zest of one organic lemon
1 1/2 cups finely chopped dried black figs
1 cup raisins
1/2 cup dark agave
2 droppers Liquid Stevia Valencia Orange
1 cup pecans
2 teaspoons cinnamon
1/2 teaspoon allspice

FROSTING
1 1/2 cups Swerve sugar substitute, powdered
2 tablespoons vegetable shortening
2 tablespoons almond milk, unsweetened soy milk, or water
1 dropper Liquid Stevia Vanilla Creme
2 teaspoons light agave
1 teaspoon beet, strawberry, or spinach baking powder

For dough: In stand up mixer with paddle attachment, cream shortening and yacon powder or Swerve. (See note for yacon powder). Add in eggs, vanilla, and salt and beat until smooth. The batter will appear curdled. Make sure to continually scrape down sides of bowl with spatula.

In separate bowl, sift together gluten-free flour, potato starch, baking powder, baking soda, Stevia Powder, and xanthan gum. In stand up mixer with paddle attachment, slowly blend in pre-sifted flour mixture into wet mixture. Knead dough with spray-oiled hands until smooth and workable. Wrap dough in plastic and chill for 2 hours.

For filling: In food processor, puree chopped orange, sliced apple, and lemon zest. One at a time, slowly add figs, raisins, agave, and Liquid Stevia by pulse action and then puree. Next pulse in pecans, allspice, and cinnamon and then puree. Add extra water to thin if needed. Should make a thick paste.

For cookies: Preheat oven to 375 degrees. Between two pieces of floured wax paper, roll out a third of the dough into a 5 inch by 10 inch rectangle shape about 1/4 inch thick. Use a floured knife to shape rectangle and cut off extra dough. Using 4 - 5 rounded tablespoons, put fig mixture in a line leaving a 1/2 inch margin from the left side. Wrap dough over mixture to your right, sealing figs inside dough. This dough is very pliable and can be rolled out many times.

With clean and floured knife, cut cookies about 1 1/2 inches, using a diagonal cut. Wipe the knife clean after every cut. Make small diagonal slits in the sides of the cookies. With spatula, move to a non-greased cookie sheet and bake for 10-12 minutes. Cool on wire rack.

For frosting: To make powdered Swerve, place Swerve in high powered blender for about five seconds and then measure 1 1/2 cups. In stand up mixer with paddle attachment, cream together powdered Swerve and vegetable shortening. Add in milk or water, Liquid Stevia, agave, and beet powder or strawberry powder for pink frosting and spinach powder for green frosting until smooth. Repeat recipe if more frosting is needed. Frost on cooled cookies.

Note: To make yacon powder from yacon slices, make sure your high-powered blender is completely dry. I heat mine up by blowing a hair dryer into it before I grind the slices to make sure no moisture is left. After I grind about two cups, I put the yacon through a sifter and then discard the small amount leftover. There will be about one to two tablespoons that won't go through the sifter. Sifting makes the yacon separate, and act like sugar. Yacon slices and/or baking powder may be order in kilo bags at www.macaweb.com.

Yield: Three dozen cookies.

cut out sugar cookie

A frosted caky, cut-out cookie made with agave -- no sugar, no wheat, and no gluten.

DOUGH
1 cup vegetable shortening
1/2 cup Swerve sugar alternative
2 eggs
1 tablespoon vanilla
1 cup sour cream
1/2 cup light agave
2 droppers Liquid Stevia Vanilla Creme
3 cups gluten-free flour
1 cup white rice flour
1 cup potato flour
4 packets or 2 teaspoons Stevia Plus Powder
2 teaspoons baking powder
1 teaspoon baking soda
1 teaspoon xanthan gum

ICING
1 cup Swerve sugar alternative, powdered
2 teaspoons unsweetened almond milk
1 dropper Liquid Stevia Vanilla Crème
2 teaspoons light agave
2 teaspoons beet, strawberry, spinach baking powder

For cookies: With paddle attachment in stand up mixer, cream shortening and Swerve. Add in eggs and beat until fluffy. Add in vanilla, sour cream, agave, and Liquid Stevia and blend.

In separate bowl, sift together gluten-free flour, white rice flour, potato flour, Stevia Powder, baking powder, baking soda, and xanthan gum.

With paddle attachment in stand up mixer, add pre-sifted dry ingredients to wet ingredients and mix. Scrape down sides of bowl. If needed, add a bit of flour to hands first and then form dough into a ball. Wrap in plastic. Refrigerate 2 hours or over night for best results to firm up dough.

Between two floured sheets of wax paper, roll out dough to about 1/4 inch thick. Peel the top layer of wax paper off dough. Cut out cookies with floured cookie cutters and place on ungreased cookie sheet. This dough is very durable and can be rolled out many times.

Bake at 350 degrees for 6-8 minutes. Depending on how thick or thin you roll the dough will depend on long you bake the cookies. Watch cookies carefully. The cookies should not brown or even be golden, but will appear white when they are done. Cookies are done when spring back to the touch. Cool on wire rack.

For frosting: To make powdered Swerve, place Swerve in a high powdered blender and blend on high for about five seconds then measure 1 cup. In stand up mixer with paddle attachment, mix well Swerve, milk or water, Liquid Stevia, agave, and fruit or vegetable powder for coloring. Beat icing for 2-3 minutes until glossy. Frost cookies with icing when cooled.

Yield: Five dozen cookies.

sicily biscotti

A fudgey, caffeine-free mocha tasting Italian cookie made with roasted maca and agave.

1/2 cup grain sweetened chocolate chips, melted
2 cups gluten-free flour
1 1/4 cups brown rice flour
2 teaspoons Stevia Plus Powder
1 teaspoon xanthan gum
1/2 teaspoon baking soda
1/2 teaspoon baking powder
dash sea salt
1/2 cup vegetable butter, slightly softened
1/2 cup Swerve sugar alternative
2 Omega 3 organic eggs
1/2 cup dark agave
1 tablespoon vanilla
1/2 cup almond meal
2 tablespoons roasted maca
1 1/2 cups organic roasted almonds, chopped

IOn medium heat in double boiler, melt chips. Set aside. In medium bowl, sift together gluten-free flour, brown rice flour, Stevia Powder, xanthan gum, baking soda, baking powder, and salt. Set aside.

With paddle attachment in stand up mixer, cream the vegetable butter until white. Add the Swerve sugar alternative and beat until fluffy, about 5 minutes. Blend in the eggs, one at a time. Add agave, vanilla, melted chips, and maca. Stir in the nuts. With paddle attachment, slowly incorporate the dry ingredients to form a firm dough. Wrap dough in plastic wrap and refrigerate dough overnight.

Preheat the oven to 375 degrees. Lightly grease two cookie sheets and line with parchment paper. Divide the dough into 3 equal pieces.

On a floured sheet of wax paper, roll each piece with hands into a log 2 inches thick and 12 inches long. Place 2 logs on one prepared baking sheet, and one log on the second prepared baking sheet, leaving enough space between them for the dough to spread while baking. Bake the logs for 20 minutes.

Let baked logs sit for 10 minutes. With serrated knife, slice the logs on a slight diagonal about 3/4 inch thick. Place the slices, cut side down on the original cookie sheets lined with parchment paper.

Lower the oven temperature to 350 degrees. Bake the slices for 12-15 minutes. Cool on a wire rack. Store in an airtight container.

Roasted Maca: To purchase roasted maca go to www.healthywiseorganics.com or check your local health food store.

Yield: Three dozen cookies.

breads pancakes and cereals

queen quinoa

wicked peanut butter waffles

it’s a piece of corn cake

eve’s apple cake

blueberry breakfast bread

star buckwheat pancakes

pumpkin spice pancakes

chocolate/carob ginger bread

the other white loaf

bean town brown bread

cinnamon twist and shout roll up

kookoo cocoa cereal

great low fat vanilla granola

queen quinoa

A gluten-free, gourmet breakfast that has high protein and stays with you all morning.

1/2 cup organic apple cider or juice
1/2 cup water
1/3 cup Ancient Harvest quinoa flakes
1 packet or 1/2 teaspoon Stevia Plus Powder
1 teaspoon pumpkin spice or cinnamon
1/2 cup organic sliced strawberries
2 teaspoons organic unsweetened coconut
1 tablespoon sliced almonds
dollop of unsweetened almond milk

In medium saucepan, bring apple cider and water to a boil. Add in quinoa flakes, Stevia Plus, and spice. At a low boil stirring constantly, cook for 90 seconds to two minutes.

Transfer cooked quinoa to a medium cereal bowl. Garnish with strawberries, coconut, almonds, and a splash of almond milk.

Yield: 1 serving.

wicked awesome peanut butter waffles

A healthy Sunday breakfast waffle with a bold peanut butter taste.

2 1/4 cups gluten-free flour
4 teaspoons baking powder
1 teaspoon xanthan gum
3/4 cup organic creamy peanut butter
3 tablespoons light agave
1 dropper Liquid Stevia Vanilla Crème
2 Omega 3 organic eggs, beaten
2 1/4 cups unsweetened soy milk or almond milk
1/4 cup vegetable spread, melted
1/4 tsp fine Celtic Sea salt

Preheat waffle iron. When hot, lightly dust with cooking spray. Sift together flour, baking powder, and xanthan gum.

Add pre-sifted dry ingredients to stand up mixing bowl. With paddle attachment, beat slowly while adding beaten eggs, milk, Stevia, agave, and melted vegetable spread. Scrape down sides of bowl. Continue to beat in peanut butter and salt until batter is smooth.

Pour a ladle full onto waffle iron and cook until golden, about 4 minutes. Serve immediately with **Strawberry Slam** (see recipe below) and fresh sliced banana or Banana Chips.

To make Banana Chips: Thinly slice two ripe organic bananas. The thinner the better -- they will dehydrate faster. Place on mesh trays and dehydrate at 105 degrees for 8 hours or until desired crispness is achieved. I like mine crispy. Then the chips can be blended slightly in a mini-food processor and sprinkled on top of jam.

Yield: 6-7 waffles and one cup of banana chips.

strawberry slam

A fruit jam that can be used as a topping for pancakes and yogurt.

2 1/2 cup chopped organic strawberries
1/2 cup spiced organic apple cider
1 teaspoon finely grated lemon zest
1 tablespoon lemon juice
2 tablespoons light agave
2 droppers Stevia Clear liquid
2 tablespoons kuzu diluted in 1/4 cup water

Wash and cut fruit and place in food processor. Pour in cider, lemon zest, lemon juice, agave, and Liquid Stevia Clear. Puree at high speed.

In medium saucepan, pour in fruit mixture and stir over a medium heat. Slowly whisk in kuzu diluted in water until it disappears. Stirring constantly, cook fruit mixture down until thick about 10 minutes. Note: You can also use blueberries, mango, apricots, and raspberries. Frozen fruit may also be used.

Yield: 2 cups.

it's a piece of corn cake

A sweet, gluten-free Mexican corn bread spiced with cumin.

2 Omega 3 organic free-range eggs, beaten
5 oz Total Greek no-fat plain yogurt, or Greek style yogurt
1/4 cup almond milk
1 dropper Liquid Stevia Lemon Drops or Clear
3 tablespoons light agave
1/2 cup organic polenta
1/2 cup Ancient Harvest quinoa flakes
1/2 cup quinoa flour
1 teaspoon baking powder
1/2 teaspoon baking soda
3 packets or 1 1/2 teaspoons Stevia Plus Powder
1/2 teaspoon cumin
dash of sea salt
2 teaspoons organic lemon zest

Preheat oven to 350 degrees. In medium mixing bowl, beat eggs. Whisk in yogurt, almond milk, Liquid Stevia, agave and zest. Stir in polenta and then quinoa flakes one at a time. Set aside.

In separate small bowl, sift quinoa flour, baking powder, baking soda, Stevia Plus Powder, cumin, and salt,. Add pre-sifted flour mixture to wet mixture stirring gently.

Spray 8x8 glass baking dish with spray oil and dust evenly with extra quinoa or white rice flour. Bake on middle rung for 30 minutes.

Yield: 9 pieces.

eve's apple cake

A super sweet, apple spiced breakfast bread made with egg whites and gluten-free whole grains.

1 cup egg whites
1/2 ripe banana
1/2 cup unsweetened applesauce
1 organic Fuji apple, sliced
1 tablespoon organic lemon juice
1 teaspoon cinnamon
1 teaspoon pumpkin spice
1 teaspoon vanilla
1/4 cup organic raw tahini, no salt added
2 tablespoons ground, golden flax meal
4 packets or 2 teaspoons Stevia Plus Powder
2 tablespoons dark agave nectar
1 cup organic quinoa flakes
1 cup quinoa flour
1 teaspoon gluten-free baking powder
1/2 teaspoon baking soda
1/2 teaspoon xanthan gum

Preheat oven to 350 degrees. In food processor, puree egg whites, banana, applesauce, Fuji apple, lemon juice, cinnamon, pumpkin spice, vanilla, tahini, flax seed, Stevia Plus Powder, and agave nectar.

In small bowl, blend quinoa flakes, quinoa flour, baking powder, baking soda, and xanthan gum. Slowly add pre-mixed dry ingredients to wet mixture. Let stand a few minutes so that the quinoa flakes absorb all the liquid.

Lightly spray oil a glass Pyrex 8x8 baking dish and lightly flour with extra quinoa flour. Spoon in mixture and spread evenly with spray oiled spatula. Bake for 35-40 minutes.

Yield: 9 pieces.

blueberry breakfast bread

A sweet breakfast bread that is low in calorie and high in whole grain fiber and protein.

1 cup egg whites
4 tablespoons light agave
2 tablespoons lemon juice
1/2 cup organic unsweetened apple sauce
4 packets or 2 teaspoons Stevia Plus Powder
1 teaspoon cinnamon
1/2 cup buckwheat groats, ground
1/2 cup quinoa flakes
1/2 cup quinoa flour
1 teaspoon baking powder
1/2 teaspoon baking powder
1/2 teaspoon xanthan gum
1 cup fresh or frozen organic blueberries
2 teaspoons quinoa flour

Preheat oven to 350 degrees. In medium bowl, whisk together egg whites, agave, lemon juice, applesauce, Stevia Plus, and cinnamon. Stir in quinoa flakes. Allow to sit for a minute. They will puff up and soak in the liquid.

In coffee grinder, grind buckwheat groats until powdered. In small bowl, sift together ground buckwheat groats, quinoa flour, baking powder, baking soda, and xanthan gum. Add pre-mixed dry ingredients to wet mixture.

Carefully dredge blueberries in 2 teaspoons quinoa flour and add to wet mixture. Pour mixture in an 8x8 prepared glass baking dish that has been spray oiled and floured with quinoa flour. Bake for 30-35 minutes.

Yield: 16 pieces.

star buckwheat pancakes

A sugar-free, gluten-free high protein pancake that is great for work outs on the go.

1 cup egg whites
1 cup buckwheat groats, ground
1/2 ripe banana
1/2 cup unsweetened almond milk
1 teaspoon cinnamon
1/2 teaspoon Stevia Plus powder

In coffee grinder, grind buckwheat groats until fine. In a blender, puree egg whites, ground groats, banana, almond milk, cinnamon, and Stevia Plus. On medium/low heat, pour pancake batter onto sprayed oiled coated griddle or Teflon coated frying pan. Cook for several minutes on eat side. Reduce heat when needed. Remember you are cooking egg whites that can burn easily.
Serving Suggestion: Serve with a bit of agave or fruit jam.

Yield: 8 pancakes.

pumpkin spice pancakes

A high protein low fat pancake made with yam that can be eaten for a dessert, snack, or breakfast.

1 cup egg whites
1/2 cup buckwheat groats, ground
1 cup baked yam
2-3 unsweetened almond milk
1 teaspoon pumpkin spice
2 droppers Liquid Stevia Vanilla Creme

In coffee grinder, grind buckwheat groats until fine. In a blender, puree egg whites, groats, yam, water, spice, and Liquid Stevia. On medium/low heat, pour pancake batter onto sprayed oiled coated griddle or Teflon coated frying pan. Cook for several minutes on each side. Reduce heat when needed.

Yield: 12 pancakes.

chocolate carob ginger bread

This chocolate ginger breakfast bread tastes like a winter spiced chocolate cake.

1/2 cup baked yam with skin
1 teaspoon fresh ginger, minced
1 cup soaked buckwheat groats
3 teaspoons Stevia Plus Powder
3 tablespoons dark agave
2 Omega 3 organic eggs
2 teaspoons cinnamon
1/2 teaspoon powdered ginger
3 rounded tablespoons roasted carob
1 rounded tablespoon unsweetened cocoa
1/2 cup plus 2 tablespoons unsweetened almond milk
1/4 cup quinoa flour
1 teaspoon baking powder
1/2 teaspoon baking soda
1 teaspoon xanthan gum

Soak 3/4 cups dry groats in 2 cups water over night. When soaking is complete, the groats will measure 1 cup.

Preheat oven to 350 degrees. In food processor, puree yam, ginger, soaked buckwheat groats, Stevia Plus, agave, eggs, cinnamon, powdered ginger, carob, and cocoa. Through spout in the food processor, slowly add almond milk while you continue to puree.

In small bowl, sift together quinoa flour, baking powder, baking soda, and xanthan gum. Add prepared dry ingredients to wet mixture in food processor and puree a few seconds. Add optional 1/4 cup raw cacao nibs if desired.

Spray oil an 8x8 glass baking dish and dust bottom of dish with quinoa flour or white rice flour. Spoon in mixture with an oiled sprayed spatula and spread evenly. Continue to use a bit of spray oil on the back of the spatula as needed for spreading. Bake for 30-35 minutes or until a knife clears the center of the bread.

Yield: 16 pieces.

the other white loaf

A homemade sugar-free/wheat-free/gluten-free white sandwich bread.

1 cup white rice flour
1 cup gluten-free flour
1/2 cup potato starch (not flour)
1/2 cup tapioca starch
2 teaspoons xanthan gum
2 1/4 tablespoons active dry yeast
1/4 teaspoon salt
1 tablespoon ground golden flax meal
3 organic Omega 3 eggs
2 tablespoons Swerve sugar alternative
1/4 cup grape seed oil
1 teaspoon apple cider vinegar
1 cup unsweetened soy milk
2 tablespoons ground golden flax to line bottom of pan

In stand up mixer, sift together white rice flour, gluten-free flour, potato starch, tapioca starch, xanthan gum, yeast, and salt. Mix in ground flax.

In separate bowl, whisk together eggs, Swerve, oil, vinegar, and soy milk. With paddle attachment on low, slowly pour wet ingredients into pre-sifted dry ingredients and beat on high for 3 minutes.

Lightly spray-oil an 8 1/2 x 4 1/2 inch bread pan. Line with parchment paper. Sprinkle 2 tablespoons flax meal on bottom of paper.

Using a large spray-oiled spatula, scrape down sides of bowl. Spray-oil again your spatula and spoon dough into prepared bread pan. Smooth top with oiled fingers or spray-oiled spatula. Cover with spray-oiled plastic wrap. Let rise in a warm place until dough reaches top of pan about 2 hours.

Cover dough in baking pan with foil tent. Bake on middle rack for 35 minutes. Take out of oven and remove foil tent. Lift bread out of pan and bake on parchment for another three-five minutes. Bread is done with golden and sounds hollow when tapped. Remove parchment. Cool on wire rack.

Yield: One loaf.

bean town brown bread

A brown bread made with black beans and quinoa and travels well on camping trips.

1 cup quinoa flour
3 teaspoons Stevia Plus Powder
1/2 teaspoon baking powder
1 teaspoon baking soda
1/2 teaspoon salt
2 teaspoons cinnamon
1/2 teaspoon allspice
1/2 cup cornmeal
3/4 cup organic black beans, drained
1/2 cup baked yam
3 tablespoons roasted carob
4 tablespoons dark agave
1 cup buttermilk
1/2 cup raisins dredged in 1 tablespoon gluten-free flour

Spray oil and gluten-free flour three empty and clean, 15 oz fruit or vegetable cans. In medium bowl, sift together quinoa flour, Stevia Plus Powder, baking powder, baking soda, salt, cinnamon, and allspice. Stir in corn meal. Set aside.

In food processor, purée beans, yam, carob, and agave. Add buttermilk slowly through spout in food processor. Add in prepared dry ingredients and pulse until mixed. Pulse in raisins dredged in flour. Spoon batter into prepared cans leaving at least two inches from top of can for breathing room. Cover with a double piece of oiled foil, dull side up and tie foil with twine or rubber band.

Put a rack or open metal vegetable steamer in an 8-quart soup pot and fill half way with water. Place cans on top of rack or metal streamer. Bring water to a boil and lower to a simmer. Cover pot and steam for two hours. Check water lever often and add more water when needed.

Remove cans and take foil off. When cool enough to handle, tip upside down and bread will slide out. Cool on wire rack.

Yield: Three loaves of bread.

cinnamon twist and shout roll ups

A sugar-free/wheat-free/gluten-free cinnamon breakfast bun with a sweet vanilla glaze.

DOUGH
2 cups gluten-free flour
1 cup potato flour (not starch)
1/4 cup tapioca starch
3 teaspoons Stevia Plus Powder
1 teaspoon baking powder
1 1/2 tablespoons dry active yeast
1/2 teaspoon salt
3 tablespoons grape seed oil
1 teaspoon vanilla
1 large egg
1 cup unsweetened soy or almond milk
2-3 tablespoons water if needed for moistening dough
extra grape seed oil for greasing

FILLING
1/3 cup light agave
4 tablespoons gluten-free flour
2 teaspoons cinnamon
2 large organic Fuji apples, chopped
1 tablespoon plus 2 teaspoons lemon juice
1 1/2 cups organic walnuts

GLAZE
1/3 cup light agave
4 tablespoons Swerve sugar alternative
1 teaspoon vanilla
3 tablespoons heavy cream
1 teaspoon kuzu dissolved in 1 tablespoon water

For dough: In stand up mixer, sift together gluten-free flour, potato flour, tapioca starch, Stevia Plus Powder, baking powder, yeast, and salt.

In separate bowl, whisk together the oil, vanilla, egg whites, and milk. With a paddle attachment on low, add prepared wet mixture to pre-sifted dry ingredients in stand up mixer until a loose dough forms. Let the dough rest for 10 minutes. This resting period allows the gluten-free flour to absorb the liquid fully.

Knead the dough for a few minutes. Add 1-2 tablespoons of water if the dough feels firm or dry. Grease hands with grape seed oil and place the dough in a greased bowl of grape seed oil, turning to coat. Cover the bowl with spray oiled plastic wrap, and let the dough rise in a warm area and let dough rise about two hours.

For filling: In food processor, puree agave, cinnamon, apples, lemon juice and walnuts for ten seconds to make a filling that can be spread evenly onto rolled out dough.

For assembly: Gently deflate the risen dough and turn it out onto a lightly white rice floured parchment paper on top of your work surface. Fold dough over once or twice to remove the excess gas. If dough is a bit dry, add 1-2 tablespoons water to hands and knead dough a few times. Divide the dough into quarters. Roll the first quarter into a 6 x 10 inch rectangle. Spread 1/4 of the filling over the rolled-out dough. Leave 1/2 inch margins.

Starting with the length side on the left, roll the dough to the right into a log, sealing the edge underneath with a bit of water on your fingers. Use a sharp, serrated knife to cut the log in six, 1 1/2 -inch rounds. Place the rounds, seam side down, side-by-side on a parchment-lined baking sheet. Repeat this process with the rest of the dough and filling.

Place a large piece of foil under baking sheet and tent over edges to avoid burning. Bake in a preheated 350 degree oven for 30-35 minutes. Let cool on wire rack for at least an hour.

For glaze: In small saucepan, whisk together agave, Swerve, vanilla, and cream, and heat to just under a slight boil. Add in dissolved kuzu in water. Stir constantly for the next 5 minutes. Remove from heat and let cool. Drizzling glaze over cooled cinnamon rolls.

Yield: 24 rolls.

kookoo cocoa cereal

A chocolate/carob cereal made with sprouted buckwheat and puffed rice.

3 cups sprouted buckwheat
1/2 cup dark agave
1/4 cup unsweetened almond milk
4 droppers Liquid Stevia Dark Chocolate
2 tablespoons unsweetened cocoa
2 tablespoons roasted carob powder
1/4 teaspoon cinnamon
3 cups unsweetened puffed rice
1/2 cup chopped organic dry roasted almonds
unsweetened almond or soy milk for eating cereal

To sprout buckwheat: Start two days before. Soak 2 cups raw buckwheat groats in 5 cups water over night. Drain groats in a large colander. Press the groats up against the sides of the colander spreading evenly. Use a plate underneath to catch the drippings. Cover with plastic wrap and let sprout for 24-36 hours in a dry, warm place. Little tails with grow the size of 1/8 inch. After buckwheat has sprouted, then measure the amount you need.

For cereal: In large bowl, mix agave, almond milk, and Liquid Stevia. Whisk in cocoa, carob, and cinnamon until smooth. In separate bowl, place puffed rice and pour 1/4 cup of wet cocoa mixture on top. Next add in 1/4 cup of chopped nuts to puffed rice mixture. Toss and place immediately on Teflex sheet spreading mixture evenly and as flat as possible for even dehydration.

In second mixing bowl, place sprouted buckwheat and pour in the rest of cocoa mixture. Add in the rest of the almonds and toss. Repeat the same process of transferring batter onto new Teflex sheet.

Dehydrate both sheets of cereal at 110 degrees. The buckwheat will dry for 16 hours. The puffed rice with dehydrate faster than buck-wheat so pull out the puffed rice at 8 hours. When both are done, mix the two cereals together breaking up the buckwheat into bite size pieces. Scoop out a cupful into in a cereal bowl and dollop with your choice of milk.

Yield: Makes 6-7 cups. Store in an airtight container. Cereal will keep for 30 days.

great low fat vanilla granola

A gluten-free granola made with sprouted buckwheat, Goji berries, raisins, and agave.

2 cups sprouted buckwheat groats
1/2 cup raisins
1/4 cup Goji berries
4 tablespoons agave
2 droppers Liquid Stevia Vanilla Creme
1 teaspoon vanilla
1 teaspoon cinnamon or pumpkin spice

To soak and sprout buckwheat. Soak 1 cup dry buckwheat groats in 2 1/2 cups filtered water overnight in your refrigerator. In the morning, drain in big colander. You may use buckwheat soaked or continue to sprout. To sprout: use spatula to press the buckwheat groats to the sides of the colander so there is an even amount around the colander. Place on top of a plate to catch water from dripping out and cover with Glad Wrap. Cut holes in plastic wrap with knife and set to sprout out of the sun in a cool dry place. Within 24-36 hours, the buckwheat will sprout baby tails (1/8 "). That's when you know it's done. Place in a container and refrigerate until use.

Note: You will have over one cup of sprouted buckwheat so measure the two cups before you start the recipe.

For granola: Mix two cups sprouted buckwheat groats, 1/2 cup soaked raisins, 1/4 cup Goji berries, 4 tablespoons agave, 1 teaspoon vanilla, 2 droppers Liquid Stevia Vanilla Creme, and 1 teaspoon cinnamon or pumpkin spice. Stir and spread onto dehydrator sheet and dehydrate at 105 degrees for 12-16 hours.

Yield: 3-4 cups dry granola. Store in an airtight container. Cereal will keep for 30 days.

muffins bagels and scones

break the fast muffins

courageous carrot cake muffins

carob chip scones

blueberry cornbread muffins

wholly cinnamon raisin bagel

magic muffins w/great ganache

break the fast muffins

A sweet gluten-free, carob muffin made with high protein flours, buckwheat groats, and agave.

2 Omega 3 eggs beaten
1/2 cup Greek style yogurt
2 tablespoons sunflower or grape seed oil
1/2 cup organic unsweetened applesauce
1/2 cup carob powder
1/2 cup ground buckwheat groats
1/3 cup quinoa flakes
3/4 cup quinoa flour
4 packets or 2 teaspoons Stevia Plus Powder
1 teaspoon cinnamon
1 teaspoon gluten-free baking powder
1/2 teaspoon baking soda
1 teaspoon xanthan gum
3/4 cup unsweetened carob chips

Preheat oven to 350 degrees. In stand up mixer with paddle attachment, beat eggs. And in yogurt,oil, and applesauce and mix well. Blend in carob powder. Set aside.

To grind buckwheat groats, place in a coffee grinder and grind buckwheat groats until fine. Place ground groats in a small bowl. With a fork or small whisk, mix in quinoa flakes, quinoa flour, Stevia Plus, cinnamon, baking powder, baking soda, and xanthan gum.

Slowly add prepared flour mixture to wet mixture in stand up mixing bowl. Set aside for a few minutes so that the quinoa flakes can absorb the rest of the liquid.

Stir in carob chips. Spoon in to muffin tins lined with paper liners or spray oiled silicon muffin trays about three quarters of the way fill. Bake for 25-30 minutes or until the center of the muffin clears a toothpick.

Yield: Makes 12 medium muffins.

courageous carrot cake muffins

An awesome carrot muffin with plump spicy raisins.

1/2 cup organic unsweetened applesauce
1 tablespoon lemon juice
1/2 cup fresh carrot juice
2 teaspoons or 4 packets Stevia Plus Powder
2 droppers Liquid Stevia Vanilla Creme
1/2 cup raisins
1 teaspoon pumpkin spice
1 teaspoon cinnamon
2 teaspoons arrowroot powder
2 eggs
1 tablespoon sunflower or grape seed oil
4 tablespoons agave nectar
1 cup processed carrots
1 cup quinoa flour
3/4 cup quinoa flakes
1 teaspoon gluten-free baking powder
1 teaspoon baking soda
1 teaspoon xanthan gum
2 teaspoons arrowroot

Preheat oven to 350 degrees. Over medium heat in a medium saucepan, add applesauce, lemon juice, carrot juice, Stevia Plus, Liquid Stevia, raisins, pumpkin spice, and cinnamon until just under a boil. Whisk in arrowroot until well blended and cook down liquid stirring constantly for another 10 minutes or until a wooden spoon can clear the bottom of the saucepan.

In stand up mixer with paddle attachment, beat eggs, oil, and agave. Stir in processed carrots. Add reduced carrot juice mixture and blend.

In small bowl, mix well the quinoa flour, flakes, baking soda, baking powder, xanthan gum, and arrow root.

Add pre-mixed dry ingredients to wet mixture and blend with paddle attachment. Let batter stand a few minutes to allow the quinoa flakes to soak in the rest of the liquid.

Spoon batter in paper lined cup cake tins or spray oiled silicon muffin trays about three quarters full. Bake for 25-30 minutes. Cool on wire rack.

Yield: 12 medium muffins.

carob chip scones

A light, gluten-free scone made with carob chips and agave.

1 1/2 cups gluten-free baking flour
1 cup quinoa flour
1 tablespoon baking powder
1/2 teaspoon baking soda
1 teaspoon xanthan gum
1 teaspoon cinnamon
2 teaspoons Stevia Plus Powder
dash salt
1/2 cup vegetable shortening
1 Omega 3 organic egg
3/4 cup unsweetened soy or almond milk
1 tablespoon vanilla
4 tablespoons dark agave
2 droppers Liquid Stevia Vanilla Creme
2 droppers Liquid Stevia Milk Chocolate
3/4 cup unsweetened carob chips
1 tablespoon gluten-free flour
extra dark agave for topping

Preheat an ungreased baking pan in 400 degree oven. In stand up mixer, sift gluten-free flour, quinoa flour, baking powder, baking soda, xanthan gum, cinnamon, Stevia Powder, and salt. Cut in vegetable shortening with pastry cutter or a fork until flour resembles little balls the size of peas.

In separate bowl, whisk together egg, soy milk, and Liquid Stevias. In stand up mixer with paddle attachment, add wet ingredient into already prepared dry ingredients. Be careful to not overwork dough. Gluten-free dough is naturally sticky.

Dredge unsweetened carob chips in gluten free flour. Toss to lightly coat chips. Next, mix in chips carefully into dough. Spoon heaping tablespoons of dough onto heated baking pan. Drizzle a teaspoon of dark agave on each scone in a crisscross pattern.

Lower oven heat to 350 degrees. Bake for 15-20 minutes. Cool on wire rack.

Yield: One dozen scones.

blueberry cornbread muffins

A sugar-free/wheat-free cornbread muffin with blueberries and agave.

2 Omega 3 organic free-range eggs, beaten
5 oz Total Greek no-fat plain yogurt, or Greek style yogurt
1/4 cup unsweetened almond milk
1 tablespoon vanilla
3 tablespoons light agave
1/2 cup organic cornmeal
1/2 cup Ancient Harvest quinoa flakes
1/2 cup quinoa flour
1/2 cup all-purpose gluten-free flour
1 teaspoon baking powder
1/2 teaspoon baking soda
4 packets or 2 teaspoons Stevia Plus Powder
one cup organic blueberries fresh or frozen
2 teaspoons gluten free flour

Preheat oven to 350 degrees. In medium mixing bowl, beat eggs. Whisk in yogurt, almond milk, vanilla and agave. Stir in cornmeal and then quinoa flakes one at a time. Set aside.

In separate small bowl, sift quinoa flour, gluten-free flour, baking powder, baking soda, and Stevia Plus Powder. Add pre-sifted flour mixture to wet mixture stirring gently.

In small bowl, toss blueberries with 2 teaspoons gluten free flour. Add dredged berries to wet mixture and gently in berries with a spatula.

Spoon batter in paper lined cup cake tins or spray oiled silicon muffin trays about three quarters full. Bake on middle rung for 30 minutes. Cool on wire rack.

Yield: 9 pieces.

wholly cinnamon raisin bagel

A homemade, sugar-free/gluten-free cinnamon raisin bagel.

2 cups gluten-free flour
1/2 cup white rice flour
1/2 cup tapioca starch
1 teaspoon Stevia Plus powder
2 teaspoons cinnamon
1/2 teaspoon salt
1 tablespoon xanthan gum
1 tablespoon yeast
1 tablespoon ground golden flax seed
2 large egg whites
2 tablespoons light agave
2 tablespoons grape seed oil
1 teaspoon coconut vinegar
1 cup warm water
1/2 cup organic raisins
1 tablespoon gluten-free flour
1/4 cup corn meal
2 tablespoons agave
extra grape seed oil for greasing hands
spray oil for greasing spatula

Line a large baking sheet with parchment paper and sprinkle corn meal on top evenly. Set aside. In stand up mixer, sift together gluten-free flour, white rice flour, tapioca starch, Stevia powder, cinnamon, salt, gum, and yeast. Stir in flax.

In separate bowl, mix egg whites, agave, oil, vinegar, and warm water. Using paddle attachment, slowly add in liquids into pre-sifted dry ingredients. Beat on high for 3-4 minutes. Gently fold in raisins dredged in flour.

Spray oil large spatula to scrape down sides of bowl. Spray-oil a large spoon to scoop out dough. Place dough on baking sheet with parchment paper covered in corn meal. Grease hands and shape into a ball. Flatten slightly with palm and using you clean and greased index finger, make a hole in the center, about the size of a pea. You may also use greased fingers to smooth out rough edges of dough.

Do this process with the rest of the dough until you make 8 bagels total. Lightly cover prepared bagels with a spray-oiled piece of plastic wrap. Allow bagels to rise for one-two hours, or until they have doubled in size.

In large skillet, bring 2 1/2 inches of water to a boil. Add in 2 tbsp agave. Once bagels have risen, drop 2 to 3 bagels in the boiling water.

Boil for 30 seconds and then flip over and cook another 30 seconds. Using a flat strainer or slotted spoon, remove bagels and put back onto same baking sheet lined with parchment paper.

Bake in a preheated oven at 375 degrees for 25-30 minutes. Cool on wire rack. Serve with almond butter and agave.

Note: This gluten-free dough is very sticky. Use oil generously on hands to handle dough.

Yield: 8 large bagels.

magic muffins with great ganache

Sugar-free/wheat-free peanut butter muffins with chocolate fudge ganache topping.

MUFFINS
3/4 cup of vegetable butter, softened
1/2 cup organic smooth peanut butter
1/2 cup Swerve sugar alternative
1 tablespoon vanilla
2 droppers Liquid Stevia Vanilla Creme
1/2 cup light agave
2 large Omega 3 eggs
1 cup sweet sorghum flour
1 cup quinoa flour
3 teaspoons Stevia Plus Powder
2 teaspoons baking powder
2 teaspoons xanthan gum
1/2 teaspoon sea salt
3/4 cup unsweetened almond milk

GANACHE
1 cup grain sweetened chocolate chips
1/2 cup heavy cream
2 tablespoons light agave
2 droppers Liquid Stevia Milk Chocolate
1/4 cup unsalted butter or vegetable butter, softened
3 tablespoons Swerve sugar alternative
1 tablespoon kuzu dissolved in 2 tablespoons cold water

For muffins: Preheat oven to 375 degrees. Line muffin tin with foil liners or use large silicon muffin tins for best results.

In stand up mixer, cream butter and peanut butter. Cream in Swerve. Add vanilla, Liquid Stevia, and agave. Beat for about 3 minutes. Add eggs one at a time and beat until smooth.

In separate bowl, sift together the sorghum flour, quinoa flour, Stevia Powder, baking powder, xanthan gum, and salt. In stand up mixer, alternate adding pre-sifted dry ingredients with almond milk into wet ingredients in mixer starting and ending with dry. Scrap down sides of bowl when needed. Pour batter into liners almost to the top leaving about 1/8 inch. This way the muffins will rise and be easy to dip into the ganache. Bake for 20-25 minutes or until centers clear the toothpick test. Cool on wire racks.

For ganache: Place chips in medium bowl and set aside. In medium saucepan over medium heat, stir cream, agave, liquid Stevia, butter, and Swerve until hot but just under a boil. Add dissolved kuzu in cold water and stir constantly until thick. Pour cream mixture over prepared chocolate chips and stir until melted. Let cool completely.

When muffins have cooled, tip muffins upside down and dip into ganache. Let excess drip off before flipping right side up. Let ganache set for 10 minutes before serving. Keep muffins refrigerated.

Yield: 12 large muffins.

candy and bars

love dove cupid candies

hemp ball truffles

hemp protein raw bar

kashi haystacks

peanut butter cups

spanish peanut popcorn balls

cherry bombs

hearts in dark chocolate

love dove cupid candies

A sugar-free, Almond Joy candy made with coconut oil, carob, almonds, and agave.

1 1/2 cups melted extra virgin coconut oil
1/4 cup organic raw almond butter
1 dropper Liquid Stevia Vanilla Creme
1 dropper Liquid Stevia Milk Chocolate
4 tablespoons agave nectar
1 tablespoon organic vanilla
6 packets or 3 teaspoons Stevia Plus Powder
2 teaspoons cinnamon
3/4 cup roasted carob powder
1/4 cup organic hemp seeds
1/4 cup almond meal
1/4 cup unsweetened coconut

To melt coconut oil, place jar under warm water or scoop out measured amount and heat slightly on stove top.

In a medium bowl, place melted coconut oil and almond butter. Stir until both are blended. Next, whisk in Liquid Stevia Vanilla Creme and Milk Chocolate, agave, and vanilla. Stir until Stevia Plus Powder until it blends evenly. Add in cinnamon and stir until it blends evenly. Next, slowly stir in carob a tablespoon at a time. The mixture should still be slightly runny. Add in almond meal, hemp seeds, and coconut. Now the mixture should still run off the spoon very slowly.

Spoon into mini cupcake trays lined with paper liners. Pour in mixture half way. Chill in freezer for 15 minutes. When the candies are set, pop out and store in a freezer safe container. Keep frozen!

Yield: 50 candies.

hemp ball truffles

A sweet raw, vegan carob truffle made with hemp butter and agave and rolled in hemp seeds.

1/2 cup sprouted and dehydrated buckwheat
3/4 cup organic raw organic hemp butter
1/2 cup raw carob powder
1/4 cup almond meal
1/2 cup dairy-free carob chips
1/4 cup unsweetened almond milk
4 packets or 2 teaspoons Stevia Plus Powder
2 tablespoons light agave nectar
2 tablespoons lemon juice
1 teaspoon organic vanilla
1/2 teaspoon cinnamon
1/2 cup hemp seeds

To soak, sprout, and dehydrate buckwheat groats: Soak 1/2 cup dry buckwheat groats in 1/2 cup filtered water overnight in your refrigerator. In the morning, drain in big colander. You may use buckwheat soaked or continue to sprout. To sprout -- use spatula to press the buckwheat groats to the sides of the colander so there is an even amount around the colander.

Place colander on top of a plate to catch water from dripping out and cover with plastic wrap. Cut holes in plastic wrap with knife and set to sprout out of the sun in a cool dry place. Within 24-36 hours, the buckwheat will sprout baby tails. That's when you know it's done. Place in a container and put into the refrigerator until use or dehydrate on Teflex sheets at 105 degrees for 12 hours.

You will have over 1/2 cup of sprouted and dehydrated buckwheat so measure your correct amount for the recipe.

To make hemp balls: In food processor, combine dehydrated buckwheat, hemp butter, carb, almond meal, carob chips, almond milk, Stevia Powder, agave, lemon juice, vanilla, and cinnamon. Form into balls and roll in hemp seeds.

Yield: 24 truffles.

hemp protein raw bar

A nutrient dense hemp protein bar made with hemp butter, raw cacao, Goji berries, and agave.

1/2 cup buckwheat groats
1 1/2 cups filtered water
1/4 cup organic ground raw cacao nibs
1/4 cup ground Goji Berries
1/2 cup hemp butter
2 droppers Liquid Stevia Dark Chocolate
1 1/2 tablespoons organic vanilla
1 teaspoon cinnamon
4 tablespoons dark agave
1/2 cup coconut date rolls
1/4 cup raw almonds
2 rounded tablespoons hemp protein powder
1/4 cup roasted carob powder
1/4 cup unsweetened almond milk
1/2 cup organic hemp seeds
3 tablespoons hemp seeds for rolling

Soak 1/2 cup buckwheat groats in 1 1/2 cups water over night, drain water well, and pat dry well with a paper towel. The buckwheat groats will have expanded to over 1/2 cup, but still use all the buckwheat. If you want, you may sprout the groats (see previous page for directions on sprouting). Set aside.

In food processor, puree cacao nibs, Goji berries, hemp butter, Liquid Stevia, vanilla, cinnamon, agave, coconut date rolls, almonds, hemp carob, and hemp seeds. Add almond milk slowly through the spout of food processor and continue processing.

Scrape down sides of food processor and repeat puree until the batter is a thick, well blended dough. Add a little extra almond milk if needed to make batter thinner so it will dough up into a ball. To test before going on, make sure the batter can be easily handled and molded into bars without sticking to your fingers. If you need to make it less sticky, add more carob.

Scoop batter out and place in mixing bowl. Fold in 1/2 cup of hemp seeds by pressing mixture against the side of the bowl with the back of a spatula or use your hands and some elbow grease. Place batter on a sheet of wax paper and mold into a flat log shape. Cut into 1/2 inch bars. Roll bars in extra hemp seeds.

Place rolled hemp bars on a Teflex dehydrator sheet and dehydrate for 18-20 hours at 105 degrees. Half way through the dehydrating time, use a spatula to remove bars from Teflex sheet, remove Teflex sheet, and place bars opposite side up on dehydrating screens for the rest of the time. This way, the bars will dry all the way through. Time may vary depending upon how chewy you want your bars.

Yield: 12 bars.

kashi haystacks

Crunchy chocolate desserts made with toasted buckwheat groats, carob chips, and agave.

1/4 cup grain sweetened chocolate chips
1/4 cup unsweetened carob chips
1 tablespoon extra virgin coconut oil
2 droppers Liquid Stevia Vanilla Creme
2 tablespoons dark agave
1 teaspoon vanilla
1 teaspoon cinnamon
1 cup dry kashi (toasted buckwheat groats)

Prepare two mini-cupcake trays with paper liners. Set aside.

In a double boiler over medium heat, melt the chocolate chips, carob chips, coconut oil, Liquid Stevia, agave, and vanilla.

When melted, stir in cinnamon and Kashi toasted buckwheat until groats are completely coated. Remove double boiler from heat.

Spoon a tablespoon of the mixture into lined mini-baking tins. Each haystack will take on its own shape when spoon dropped into the cups. Place in freezer for 10 minutes. Store in refrigerator.

Optional: Add 2 rounded tablespoons ground raw cacao nibs and 2 tablespoons Goji berries after you add in the Kashi toasted buckwheat groats.

Yield: 12 haystacks.

peanut butter cups

A sugar-free organic chocolate peanut butter cup made with agave.

CANDY
1 1/2 cups extra virgin coconut oil, melted
3/4 cup organic roasted peanut butter
1 tablespoon organic vanilla extract
3 droppers Liquid Stevia Vanilla Creme
4 tablespoons light agave nectar
3 teaspoons Stevia Plus Powder
2 teaspoons cinnamon
3/4 cup roasted carob powder
1/2 cup unsweetened cocoa powder
1/2 cup almond meal
1/2 cup hemp seeds

FILLING
1 cup organic peanut butter
3 tablespoons agave

For candy: Line mini cup cake tins with paper liners. Melt coconut oil by placing jar under hot water or spoon into saucepan and melt over low flame. When coconut oil turns to a liquid, pour oil in medium bowl. Slowly whisk in peanut butter until smooth.

Whisk in vanilla, cinnamon, Liquid Stevia, Stevia Powder, and agave nectar one at a time. Then slowly stir in carob and cocoa powder a spoonful at a time. Stir in almond meal and hemp seeds one at a time sprinkling evenly as you go. Batter should run off of spoon easily, but not too runny.

For filling: In separate bowl with a spatula, mix peanut butter and agave until smooth. It's best to use a thick peanut butter. Spoon prepared chocolate/carob batter into cup cake papers until a third filled. Spoon in a 1/2 teaspoon of the peanut butter filling on top. Pour chocolate/carob batter over peanut butter leaving space at the top of the paper liner. Chill in freezer for 15 minutes. Keep in the freezer!

Yield: approx. 50 candies.

spanish peanut popcorn balls

A sugar-free popcorn snack made with agave and Spanish peanuts.

1 cup light agave
2 tablespoons vegetable butter
1/2 cup Swerve sugar alternative
1 tablespoon kuzu
1 tablespoon cold water
2 teaspoons coconut toddy vinegar
15 cups freshly popped popcorn
1 cup Spanish peanuts

Over low/medium heat in a medium saucepan, cook agave, vegetable butter, and Swerve until thick like a syrup (just about to boil about 5 minutes). In small cup, dissolve kuzu in water and vinegar. Add to saucepan. Stir constantly until thick and reduce liquid for another 15 minutes. Remove from heat. Let cool for 5 minutes.

In 8-quart soup pot, place popcorn. Next add the peanuts. Pour wet ingredients from saucepan over popcorn and peanuts. Stir with a long wooden spoon until popcorn and peanuts are evenly coated with syrup. Let sit another 5-10 minutes to cool. If you don't, the popcorn will fall apart because it is still too warm to stick together.

Line two baking sheets with wax paper. Spray oil a one cup dry measuring cup so popcorn won't stick and scoop out a big scoop of popcorn mixture. Flip cup over and place popcorn mixture on to wax paper. Spray fingers lightly with cooking spray to keep from sticking to popcorn and mold popcorn into a tight ball with the bottom staying flat on the wax paper.

Repeat until the popcorn mixture is finished. Refrigerate popcorn balls for at least one hour to set. Keep refrigerated.

Yield: Nine, oversized one cup balls.

cherry bombs

A raw vegan dessert truffle made with cherries, Brazil nuts and coconut creme.

1/3 cup coconut cream butter
1/2 cup roasted carob
1 tablespoon unsweetened cocoa powder
2 tablespoons dark agave
2 teaspoons Stevia Plus Powder
2 droppers Liquid Stevia Dark Chocolate
1 cup pitted organic cherries, fresh or frozen
1 1/2 cups organic Brazil nuts
1/2 cup unsweetened carob chips
15 fresh cherries, pitted and halved

In food processor, puree coconut creme, carob, cocoa powder, agave, Stevia Powder, Liquid Stevia, cherries, and Brazil nuts. When dough is formed, gently pulse in carob chips. With a tablespoon, scoop out dough and form into balls. Serve in mini paper cup cake liners. Top with half cherry. Freeze for 15 minutes and serve. Keep refrigerated.

Note: Tops of cherries will get frostbite if kept in the freezer over 15 minutes.

Yield: 30 Cherry Bombs.

hearts in dark chocolate

Pineapple and strawberries dipped in sugar-free dark chocolate sauce.

one large pineapple, cut into 1/4 inch round slices
16 oz strawberries, cleaned with stem on
2 oz Scharffen Berger 99% dark, unsweetened baking cocoa bar
3 tablespoons light agave
2 droppers Liquid Stevia Dark Chocolate
1 teaspoon vanilla
2 tablespoons Swerve sugar alternative
1/4 teaspoon organic cinnamon
2 rounded tablespoons coconut crème
3 tablespoons unsweetened almond milk

For fruit: Wash and dry strawberries -- keeping stem on and place in a bowl. Set aside. Cut and trim a fresh pineapple into 1/4 inch round slices. Set aside. Line a baking sheet with parchment paper and set aside.

For dipping sauce: Over medium flame in a double boiler, melt unsweetened chocolate, agave, Liquid Stevia, vanilla, Swerve, and coconut crème. Mix until smooth. Whisk in cinnamon followed by almond milk. Mix chocolate sauce again until smooth.

Keep saucepan on stove and turn down flame to low. Dip pineapple slices and strawberries half way into the dark chocolate sauce and place on the wax paper. You may have left over fruit and may have to make another round of sauce.

Immediately place in the freezer and let set for at least 10 minutes before serving. Keep refrigerated.

Yield: Twelve, 1 cup servings.

cakes

miami beach bikini cake

lemon filled fun cake

marilyn and strawberries

voluptuous volcano cakes

mocha maca crumb cake

espresso macchiato

blueberry poundless cake

miami beach bikini cake

This is my sugar-free/wheat-free take on a winning double layer chocolate cake.

CAKE (makes one 8 inch cake)
1/2 cup grain sweetened chocolate chips
2 cups gluten-free flour
1/2 cup potato starch (not flour)
1/2 cup tapioca starch
1 teaspoon baking powder
1 teaspoon baking soda
1 teaspoon xanthan gum
2 teaspoons or 4 packets Stevia Plus Powder
1/4 teaspoon salt
2 large Omega 3 organic eggs
3 tablespoons grape seed oil
3 tablespoons water
1/2 cup chocolate rice milk
3/4 cup Swerve sugar substitute
1 tablespoon vanilla
3 droppers Liquid Stevia Milk Chocolate

TOPPING
1 cup grain sweetened chocolate chips
1 cup chopped walnuts
1/2 cup agave
2 teaspoons cinnamon
2 teaspoons Valrhona unsweetened dark cocoa powder

FROSTING
1 cup heavy cream
2 tablespoons light agave

For cake: The ingredient list make enough for one, 8 inch cake. It's best to make the first layer and then repeat the process again for the second layer.

Preheat oven to 350 degrees. In double boiler, melt 1/2 cup chips and set aside. In medium mixing bowl, sift together gluten-free flour, potato starch, tapioca starch, baking powder, baking soda, xanthan gum, Stevia Powder, and salt. Set aside.

In stand up mixing bowl using wire attachment, beat eggs, oil, water, and rice milk until fluffy about 5 minutes. Add in Swerve, vanilla, and Liquid Stevia. Beat well. With a spatula, add in melted chips. In stand up mixer, change to a paddle attachment and at low speed, add pre-sifted dry ingredients to wet mixture. Beat as little as possible.

Pour batter into a greased and floured 9 inch cake pans or ungreased silicon pans for best results. Repeat cake batter process for second layer.

For topping: In small bowl, mix chips, nuts, agave, cinnamon, and cocoa. Divide nut mixture in half and sprinkle evenly on each un-baked cake. Bake 30-35 minutes or until toothpick comes out clean. Cool on top of wire rack until cool enough to remove from pans.

For frosting: In stand up mixing bowl with wire attachment, beat heavy cream with agave until stiff about 5 minutes. Place first cake layer on a cake dish. Frost top of first cake ad sides completely. Place second cake on top and frost sides only leaving cake open face. Keep refrigerated.

Gluten-free substitute: Instead of using grain sweetened chocolate chips, melt 3 oz 99% dark unsweetened baking chocolate with 1 tablespoon light agave and 1 dropper Liquid Stevia. And for rice milk which is usually sweetened with brown rice syrup and contains gluten, use a home made almond milk or cashew milk sweetened with agave and Liquid Stevia or and unsweetened almond milk.

Yield: one double layer 9 inch cake.

lemon filled fun

Individual sugar-free/wheat-free lemon filled baby Bundt cakes.

LEMON FILLING
1/2 cup organic lemon juice
1 cup water
2 tablespoons agar agar
1 tablespoon organic lemon zest
6 tablespoon light agave
1 dropper lemon Stevia
5 tablespoons kuzu dissolved in 1/2 cup cold water

CAKE
2 cups gluten-free flour
1/2 cup potato starch (not flour)
1/2 cup tapioca starch
3 teaspoons Stevia Plus Powder
1 teaspoon baking powder
1 teaspoon baking soda
1 teaspoon xanthan gum
1/2 teaspoon salt
2 large organic Omega 3 eggs
3 tablespoons grape seed oil
3 tablespoons water
1/2 cup vanilla rice milk
1/2 cup Swerve sugar substitute
3 droppers Liquid Stevia Lemon Drops
2 tablespoons organic lemon zest
organic lemon slices for garnish

For filling: Make lemon filling the day before and keep in the fridge over night to set. In medium saucepan, whisk together lemon juice, water, agar, zest, agave, and Liquid lemon Stevia. Bring to a boil and simmer until agar is diluted. In small cup, dissolve kuzu in half cup cold water by stirring with a spoon and add to saucepan. Over medium low heat, stir until thick about 10 minutes. Transfer to a bowl. Let cool and place in fridge overnight.

For cake: Preheat oven to 350 degrees. Sift gluten-free flour, potato starch, tapioca starch, Stevia Powder, baking powder, baking soda, xanthan gum, and salt. Set aside.

In stand up mixer using wire attachment, beat eggs, oil, water, and rice milk until frothy about 5 minutes. Mix in Swerve, Liquid lemon Stevia, and zest.

In stand up mixer, change to a paddle attachment on low and add in dry pre-sifted ingredients slowly to wet ingredients. Beat as little as possible.

Pour batter in silicon, ungreased baby bunt pans about 3/4 of the way full. Let sit five minutes before placing in oven. Bake for 30-35 minutes or until cake is firm. Transfer to wire rack immediately. Cakes will slide out easily. Cool completely.

Spoon lemon filling in middle of baby bunt cake until it flows over the side of the cake and garnish with organic lemon slices.

Yield: 9 baby Bundt cakes with filling.

marilyn and strawberries

A sugar-free/gluten-free tube cake made with whipped cream and organic strawberries.

CAKE
2 1/2 cups gluten-free flour
3/4 cup potato starch
3/4 cup tapioca starch
3 teaspoons Stevia Plus Powder
2 teaspoons baking powder
1 teaspoon baking soda
2 teaspoons xanthan gum
1/2 teaspoon salt
3 large organic Omega 3 eggs
1/4 cup grape seed oil
3 tablespoons water
3/4 cup Swerve
3/4 cup vanilla rice milk
1 tablespoon vanilla extract
3 droppers Liquid Stevia Vanilla Creme
3 tablespoons strawberry baking powder
1 cup sliced strawberries tossed in 1 tablespoon light agave

FROSTING
1 cup heavy cream
2 tablespoons light agave
1 tablespoon strawberry baking powder
2 cups strawberries sliced and fanned for decorating

For cake: Preheat oven to 350 degrees. Sift together gluten-free flour, potato starch, tapioca starch, Stevia Powder, baking powder, baking soda, xanthan gum, and salt. Set aside. On high in stand up mixer using wire attachment, beat eggs, oil, and water, until fluffy and frothy about 5-7 minutes. Lower speed and mix in Swerve, rice milk, vanilla extract, vanilla liquid Stevia, and strawberry powder.

In stand up mixer, change to a paddle attachment on low and add in dry pre-sifted ingredients to wet ingredients. Beat as little as possible. In small bowl toss sliced strawberries in agave and fold strawberries gently into batter. Fold in strawberries.

Pour batter into spray oiled and gluten-free floured tube cake pan. Let sit for 5 minutes. Bake for 35-40 minutes or until an inserted toothpick comes out clean. Cool and transfer to wire rack before frosting.

For frosting: Chill mixing bowl in freezer for 20 minutes. Beat cold, heavy cream, agave, and strawberry powder until cream forms soft peaks. Frost while frosting is fresh and cold. Top with sliced strawberries. Keep cake refrigerated.

Note: Strawberry powder can be ordered from Wilderness Family Naturals at 866-936-6457.

Yield: One, 9-inch tube cake.

voluptuous volcano cakes

Individual, chocolate cakes that ooze a fudge-like chocolate filling.

3/4 cup vegetable butter
1 1/2 cups grain sweetened chocolate chips
3 large organic Omega 3 egg yolks
3 large organic Omega 3 eggs
1/2 cup Swerve sugar alternative
3 tablespoons light agave
1 tablespoon vanilla
3 droppers Liquid Stevia Dark Chocolate
1/2 cup plus 1 tablespoon cup gluten-free flour
1/4 cup tapioca starch
1/3 cup unsweetened dark cocoa powder (Valrhona)
spray oil
extra Valrhona cocoa for dusting

Preheat oven to 350 degrees. In double boiler, melt the vegetable butter and chocolate chips. Set aside to cool slightly. In stand up mixer with paddle attachment, beat eggs, egg yolks, Swerve, agave, vanilla, and Liquid Stevia on medium-high speed for about 5 minutes until mixture is thick and light yellow in color. On low speed with paddle attachment, add in the melted chocolate/butter mixture.

In small bowl, sift together gluten-free flour, tapioca starch, and cocoa powder. Gradually add the pre-sifted flour mixture to wet mixture and blend.

Butter six ramekins (6 ounces each) and dust with the extra dark cocoa powder. Tap out the excess cocoa, but make sure they are well coated. Pour the batter into the ramekins filling them about 7/8 of the way to the top.

Place on baking tray and bake for 13 minutes exactly. Check to make sure your oven temperature is correct. The cake is done when firm and the top is still soft to the touch. Remove from the oven and cool for 3 minutes. Run a paring knife between the cake and ramekin to loosen. Invert your dessert plate over the ramekin (be careful, they're hot) and flip over. Tap the plate lightly and lift off the ramekin. Garnish with raspberries.

Yield: Six individual cakes.

mocha maca crumb cake

A sweet espresso chocolate flavored coffee cake.

1 1/2 cups yacon powder or Swerve sugar substitute
1/2 cup dark agave
1/2 cup vanilla lactose-free whey protein powder
2 teaspoons cinnamon
4 packets or 2 teaspoons Stevia Plus Powder
3 droppers Liquid Stevia Cinnamon
3 droppers Liquid Stevia Dark Chocolate
3/4 cup vegetable butter
3/4 cup vegetable shortening
1 cup low fat buttermilk
1 organic Omega 3 egg
3 tablespoons roasted maca
1 teaspoon baking soda
1 teaspoon baking powder
1 teaspoon xanthan gum
1 teaspoon nutmeg
1/2 teaspoon salt

Preheat oven to 350 degrees. In medium bowl, mix yacon powder or Swerve, agave, protein powder, cinnamon, Stevia Plus Powder, Liquid Stevia Cinnamon, and Liquid Stevia Dark Chocolate.

Cut in vegetable butter and vegetable shortening with two forks or a pastry cutter until dough forms little balls the size of peas. Take out one cup of this mixture for topping and set aside.

Transfer rest of original batter to stand up mixer and with a paddle attachment, mix in buttermilk and egg. Beat a few times on low. In another separate bowl, mix together roasted maca, baking soda, baking powder, xanthan gum, nutmeg, and salt. Add prepared dry ingredients to wet mixture and beat on low. Be careful to not over beat.

Pour batter into a spray oiled and gluten-free floured 8x8 glass baking dish or baking pan. Spread topping that was set aside earlier on top of batter evenly. Use a foil over and around edges of dish to protect topping from browning to quickly. Bake for 30-35 minutes or until cake clears a toothpick. Cool in pan.

Note: To make yacon powder from yacon slices, make sure your high-powered blender is completely dry. I heat mine up by blowing a hair dryer into it before I grind the slices to make sure no moisture is left. After I grind about two cups, I put the yacon through a sifter and then discard the small amount leftover. There will be about one to two tablespoons that won't go through the sifter. Sifting makes the yacon separate, become more like a baking powder, and act like sugar. Yacon slices and/or baking powder may be order in kilo bags at www.macaweb.com.

Roasted Maca: To purchase roasted maca go to www.healthywiseorganics.com.

Yield: 16 pieces.

blueberry poundless cake

A blueberry and lemon Bundt cake with lemon sugar-free glaze.

CAKE
1 cup gluten-free flour
1 cup sweet sorghum flour
1/2 cup potato starch (not flour)
1/4 cup tapioca starch
1 1/2 teaspoons baking powder
1/2 teaspoon baking soda
2 teaspoons xanthan gum
1/4 teaspoon salt
1 teaspoon cinnamon
1 cup vegetable butter
1 3/4 cups Swerve sugar alternative
4 eggs
2 tablespoons lemon juice
1 tablespoon lemon zest
2 tablespoons vanilla extract
1 cup almond milk
1 1/2 cups blueberries dredged in 1 tablespoon gluten-free flour

GLAZE
1 1/2 cups Swerve sugar alternative, powdered
2 tablespoons lemon juice
2 tablespoons light agave
lemon peel for garnish

For cake: Preheat oven to 350 degrees. In medium bowl, sift together gluten-free flour, sorghum flour, potato starch, tapioca starch, baking powder, baking soda, xanthan gum, salt, and cinnamon. Set aside.

In stand up mixer with paddle attachment, cream butter until smooth. Add in Swerve and beat until fluffy about 2 minutes. Beat in eggs one at a time. Add lemon juice, lemon zest, and vanilla. With paddle attachment in stand up mixer, slowly beat in pre-sifted dry flour ingredients to wet mixture starting with flour and alternating with almond milk. Fold in blueberries with spatula.

For best baking results, spoon batter into a 12-cup silicon ungreased bundt pan. Spray oil a butter knife and carefully run the knife through the batter to eliminate air holes. If you use a metal Bundt pan, grease and flour the pan before spooning in batter. Bake for 45-50, or until knife tip comes out clean. Cool completely on wire rack.

For glaze: To powder Swerve, place Swerve in high powered blender on high for about five seconds. In small bowl, whisk together Swerve, lemon juice, and light agave. Drizzle on cooled cake. Garnish with lemon peel.

Yield: One Bundt cake

pies tarts and crisps

ying yang cheese cake

gran's strawberry rhubarb pie

kelly's pumpkin pie

pear and tahini creme cheese pie

peaceful pear & pomegranate tart

passionate peach crisp

yin yang cheese cake

It's balance. A dairy-free, gluten-free cheese cake made with agave, almonds, and cashews.

CRUST
1 cup coconut date rolls or 1 1/2 cups Medjool dates
3/4 cup dry Brazil nuts
1/4 cup almond meal
1 teaspoon cinnamon
dash of water or almond milk for wetness if needed

FILLING
1 cup soaked raw, organic almonds
1 cup soaked raw, organic cashews
4 tablespoons light agave nectar
1 tablespoon organic vanilla
3 droppers Liquid Stevia Vanilla Creme
1/2 cup unsweetened almond milk plus two tablespoons
1 tablespoon lemon organic lemon juice
1 teaspoon cinnamon
1/2 cup unsweetened organic coconut
3 droppers Liquid Stevia Milk Chocolate
3 rounded tablespoons carob powder

Crust: Spray 9-inch glass pie plate with non-stick spray. To make the crust, blend coconut date rolls, Brazil nuts, almond meal, cinnamon in food processor with S blade until it forms a ball. Add water or almond milk one teaspoon at a time if needed for wetness. Remove S blade from processor and transfer crust to prepared pie plate. Press down into the center of pie plate with thumb and then palm and flatten and shape dough into a pie crust. Place crust in dehydrator at 105 degrees for 6 hours. Remove from dehydrator and allow to cool

Filling: In food processor, blend almonds, cashews, agave, vanilla, Liquid Stevia Vanilla Creme, almond milk, lemon juice, cinnamon and coconut until smooth.

Note: Add more almond milk for thinner batter if necessary. To make batter super fine, transfer batter into Vita Mix and blend one cup at a time. Scoop out half the batter and transfer to a small bowl.

To food processor, add Liquid Stevia Milk Chocolate and carob into rest of mixture and blend until carob is evenly distributed. Next, assemble pie into yin yang shape.

Ying Yang shape: Cut out a 4 inch by 9 inch piece of cardboard and cover neatly with foil. Shape the foiled covered cardboard into an S-shape. Spray oil both sides of the foiled cardboard shape and place in the middle of the dehydrated prepared pie crust. Now spread the vanilla filling. Keep the S-shape foil covered cardboard in place and spread the carob filling. Gently remove foil covered cardboard and you should see a perfect ying yang/vanilla/carob shape.

Allow cheesecake to chill in refrigerator at least two hours before serving.

Yield: One, 9-inch pie.

gran's strawberry rhubarb pie

A strawberry rhubarb custard pie in a vanilla protein packed, gluten-free flakey crust.

CRUST (enough for one crust)
1 1/2 cups gluten-free baking flour
1/2 cup potato starch
1/2 cup arrow root starch
1/2 cup vanilla lactose-free whey protein powder
1 teaspoon xanthan gum
1/8 teaspoon baking powder
2 teaspoons Stevia Plus Powder
1 cup vegetable shortening
1 organic Omega 3 egg
2 tablespoons water
1 tablespoon coconut toddy or apple cider vinegar
1 egg yolk plus 1 tablespoon water to brush edges of crust

To make one crust, (you will need two): Sift together gluten-free flour, potato starch, arrow root starch, protein powder, xanthan gum, baking powder, and Stevia Powder. Cut in shortening with two forks or pastry cutter. Mixture looks like small crumbs the size of peas.

In small bowl, whisk together egg, water, and vinegar toddy. Add this to prepared flour mixture mixing well, and using hands form into a ball. Place dough on a sheet of floured wax paper.

Using extra gluten-free flour on top of dough, place another sheet of wax paper on top for rolling. Carefully roll out crust until it is big enough to fit in a 9-inch pie plate. Carefully, but quickly, remove top sheet of wax paper and flip crust into pie plate. Flute edges. If the crust breaks, this is normal. Press it back together. You will have plenty of crust left over to play with.

In custard cup, beat egg yolk and water. With pastry brush, coat fluted edges and top with an egg yolk bath.

Note: This crust recipe is enough for one crust. For best results, repeat the process to make second crust. Gluten-free dough is often flimsy and crumbly because there is no gluten to hold the dough together. Roll dough out a tiny bit thicker that a usual wheat crust. Be brave yet gentle with the dough, but at the same time don't hesitate when placing in pie plate. This is when the dough can break. If it does, patch it back together. This is normal for a gluten-free pie crust.

FILLING
4 tablespoons unsweetened almond milk
2 teaspoons kuzu
3 large organic Omega 3 eggs, beaten
1/2 cup yacon powder or Swerve sugar substitute
1/2 cup light agave
1/3 cup vanilla lactose-free whey or rice protein powder
3 tablespoons Wilderness Family Naturals strawberry powder
2 droppers Lemon Stevia Liquid Drops
1 teaspoon nutmeg
2 tablespoons gluten-free flour
2 cups rhubarb, chopped
2 cups sliced strawberries
2 tablespoons light agave
1 tablespoon lemon juice
2 tablespoons vegetable butter

To make custard filling: Preheat oven to 400 degrees. In stand up mixer with paddle attachment, place almond milk and kuzu and beat until kuzu is dissolved. Add three beaten eggs and mix. Then add yacon (see note about yacon) or Swerve sugar substitute, agave, protein powder, strawberry powder, Liquid Stevia, nutmeg, and gluten-free flour. Beat until smooth.

In medium bowl, toss chopped rhubarb and sliced strawberries in agave and lemon juice. Place prepared fruit mixture in prepared pie crust.

Pour custard mixture over fruit. Cut up vegetable butter and dot over fruit and custard filling. Place second crust on top. Flute edges. Using pastry brush, gently bathe crust with yolk.

Once pie is assembled and given an egg yolk bath, place a large piece of foil over pie and tent it around the edges of pie. This assures the gluten-free crust will not burn. Bake at 400 degrees for 50-60 minutes or until golden brown and firm. Best to let cool and then place in fridge for an hour in order for custard to set.

Note: Strawberry powder can be ordered from Wilderness Family Naturals at 866-936-6457.

Note: To make yacon powder from yacon slices, make sure your high-powered blender is completely dry. I heat mine up by blowing a hair dryer into it before I grind the slices to make sure no moisture is left fro washing. Grind about two cups and then put the yacon through a sifter. Sifting makes the yacon act like sugar. Yacon slices and/ or baking powder may be ordered in kilo bags at www.macaweb.com.

Yield: One, 9-inch pie.

kelly's pumpkin pie

A sugar-free/gluten-free spiced pumpkin pie.

PIE CRUST (enough for one crust)
1 cup gluten-free baking flour
1/2 cup potato starch
1/4 cup arrow root starch
1 teaspoon xanthan gum
1 teaspoon Stevia Plus Powder
3/4 cup Spectrum vegetable shortening
1 organic Omega 3 egg
1 egg to brush edges of fluted crust
2 tablespoons water
1 tablespoon coconut toddy

Note: Gluten-free dough is often flimsy and crumbly because there is no gluten to hold the dough together. Be brave and gentle with the dough, but at the same time don't hesitate when rolling and placing in pie plate. These are the moments the dough can break.

Sift together gluten-free flour, potato starch, arrow root, xanthan gum, and Stevia Powder. Cut in shortening with two forks or a pastry cutter is best. Mixture will look like small crumbs the size of peas. Set aside.

In small bowl, whisk together egg, water, and toddy. Add this to flour mixture mixing well and form into a ball using your hands. Place dough on a sheet of wax paper and cut into two halves and re-shape into two balls.

Place one half of the dough on the wax paper. Cover it with another sheet and carefully roll out crust until it is big enough to fit in a 9 inch pie plate. Carefully, but quickly, remove top sheet of wax paper and flip crust into pie plate. Flute edges. If the crust breaks, this is normal. Press it back together. With pastry brush, coat fluted edges of pie crust and set aside.

Continue with making pumpkin pie filling. You can use organic pumpkin by simply roasting it whole at 400 for about 45 minutes to an hour or until a knife easily clears the flesh. Let cool. Cut out a circular hole at the top, remove vine and cut pumpkin in half. Remove seeds and skin and measure the amount of pumpkin needed. Freeze the rest.

PIE FILLING
2 large organic Omega 3 eggs
1, 15 oz can organic unsweetened pumpkin, or 2 cups, fresh
1/2 cup light agave
2 tablespoons dark agave
2 droppers Vanilla Crème Stevia Liquid Drops
2 teaspoons cinnamon
2 teaspoons pumpkin spice
1/2 teaspoon powdered ginger
1/2 teaspoon nutmeg
1/2 teaspoon all spice
2 tablespoons vanilla
2 tablespoons cashew butter
2 tablespoons gluten-free flour

Pre-heat oven to 400 degrees. In stand up mixer mixer, beat eggs and then add in pumpkin, agave, liquid stevia, cinnamon, pumpkin spice, ginger, nutmeg allspice, vanilla, cashew butter, and flour. Mix well.

Pour into prepared pie-crust. Cover pie with a foil tent and bake at 400 for 15 minutes and then reduce to 350 degrees and bake for another 45 minutes or until center is set.

Yield: one, 9″ pie.

pear and tahini creme cheese pie

A pear kanten made with raw tahini and agave.

KANTEN CRUST
4 tablespoons agar agar
1 cup water
1 cup apple cider
1/2 cup raw organic almond butter or walnut butter
1 1/2 cups raw organic tahini (no salt added)
4 packets or 2 teaspoons Stevia Plus Powder
2 tablespoons dark agave
2 teaspoons cinnamon
1 tablespoon vanilla

PEAR TOPPING
3 ripe, organic Bartlett or Bosc pears
1/2 cup apple cider
1 tablespoon lemon juice
2 tablespoons light agave
4 packets or 2 teaspoons Stevia Plus Powder
1 teaspoon pumpkin spice
2 tablespoons kuzu diluted in 2 tablespoons water
1/2 cup raw walnuts, chopped

To make kanten crust: In medium sauce pan over medium heat, dissolve agar agar in 1 cup water and 1 cup apple cider by bringing liquids to a boil and then lowering heat to a simmer. Whisk in almond butter, then tahini. Stir in agave, cinnamon and vanilla. Pour agar mixture into an 8x8 Pyrex glass baking dish and chill for at least one hour.

To make topping: Peel and slice pears and place in food processor with apple cider, lemon juice, agave, Stevia Powder, and pumpkin spice. Blend until smooth. Place pear mixture in a medium sauce pan and heat over a medium flame. Mix kuzu and water until kuzu is diluted and add to pear mixture stirring constantly for about 10 minutes or until thick like a pudding.

Pour over chilled tahini pie bottom and chill for another hour. Sprinkle chopped walnuts on top.

Yield: 9 servings.

peaceful pear & pomegranate tart

A rustic, roasted pear and pomegranate tart with pistachio crust.

DOUGH
1 1/2 sticks unsalted butter
3/4 cup Swerve sugar substitute
2 large, Omega 3 organic egg yolks
1 1/4 cups gluten-free flour
1 teaspoon xanthan gum
1/8 teaspoon baking powder
1/2 teaspoon salt
1/2 cup unsalted roasted and shelled pistachios (finely ground)
2 teaspoons heavy cream
spray oil for greasing removable 11-inch tart pan

FILLING
6 firm, ripe organic Bosc pears
1/2 cup dark agave
2 tablespoons unsalted butter
1/2 heavy cream (very cold)
3 tablespoons light agave
1 cup Mascarpone cheese
1/2 cup melted and cooled coconut crème
1/2 teaspoon cinnamon
1/2 cup pomegranate seeds
2 tablespoons dark agave for drizzle

For dough: In stand up mixer with the paddle attachment, cream the butter first, then add Swerve and beat on low speed until combined, about 2 minutes. Add egg yolks and mix until well combined.

In small bowl, sift together the gluten-free flour, xanthan gum, baking powder, and salt. With paddle attachment, add pre-sifted flour to butter mixture in stand up mixer.

Grind pistachios in sturdy coffee grinder to a medium fine flour. Measure 1/2 cup of pistachios and add to stand up mixer with paddle attachment on low. Add in cream. Dough will be soft but not stick to fingers, but for easy handling, spray oil a large spoon and dot dough evenly around onto spray-oiled 11-inch removable tart pan. Place a sheet of spray-oiled plastic wrap over dough in tart pan and press down with a 10 inch cake pan to flatten. Remove cake pan and with flat edge of dry measuring cup spread dough evenly to edges of tart pan. Carefully remove plastic wrap and with fingers press dough into tiny fluted edges around tart pan. Only go to the edge of the top of the tart pan and not up and over the edge. This will ensure the crust not to break off.

After 30 minutes, remove tart shell from refrigerator. Line the shell with a piece of parchment paper slightly larger than the pan. Fill lined tart shell with the 10-inch cake pan. Place in 375 degree preheated oven and bake until edges are just beginning to turn golden brown about 15 minutes. Remove cake pan and parchment paper. Continue to bake for another 10 minutes or until crust is golden all over and looks dry. Transfer to wire rack to cool completely. After about 20 minutes, remove tart shell from pan and place on serving platter.

For filling: Cut unpeeled pears in quarters length wise, leaving one quarter with stem in tact. Do this with two of the pears and remove the stem off the rest of the pears. Core the pears and remove inner fibers. Set aside.

In a large heavy bottom saute pan over medium heat, melt vegetable butter and dark agave. Reserve a quarter of each ingredients if all the pears do not fit into sauté pan (you may have to do two rounds of pear saute).

Heat butter and agave stirring with wooden until dissolved and just beginning to bubble. Carefully place pear quarters cut side down in agave/butter caramel sauce and cook turning occasionally (with tongs) until a knife goes through flesh with ease, about 10-12 minutes. If caramel mixtures starts smoke, reduce heat to low or carefully remove pan from heat while pan cools. Pears should be tender and golden amber colored. Carefully remove pears from pan and place on baking sheet to cool completely.

In the bowl of stand up mixer beat VERY COLD heavy cream with light agave until soft peaks have formed. In another bowl gently stir the Mascarpone cheese with spatula until creamy. With spatula, gently fold in Mascarpone cheese into whipped cream in stand up mixer as to not over mix the cheese. Now with paddle attachment, stir in coconut crème and cinnamon until just combined. Do not over beat. If coconut cream is solid, it's because the temperature in your kitchen is below 76 degrees. If so, measure coconut crème and melt in a small saucepan over low heat, cool completely, and then add to cheese mixture.

Immediately assemble tart. Start with dotting prepared cheese mixture evenly into tart crust and spread with spatula. Add sliced pears length wise into fan shape in a clockwise fashion around the edges of the tart. Make another smaller inner circle with the pears fanning in the same fashion. The last two pears with stems should be placed in the middle. Sprinkle with pomegranate seeds, drizzle with extra dark agave and refrigerate until served.

Yield: Makes one 11-inch tart.

passionate peach crisp

A baked peach dessert made with organic peaches, cinnamon, nutmeg, and agave and topped with a sugar-free crumble.

2 1/2 pounds fresh peaches, peeled, pitted, and sliced
1/2 cup light agave
1 teaspoon vanilla
2 teaspoons cinnamon
1 teaspoon nutmeg
1/2 cup sifted gluten-free baking flour
1 teaspoon Stevia Plus Powder
1/2 cup oats
1/2 cup vegetable butter, softened
1/2 cup chopped pecans
2 tablespoons light for drizzle

Preheat oven to 375 degrees. Vegetable butter an 8 x 8 inch square, baking dish. In large mixing bowl, toss sliced peaches with agave, vanilla, cinnamon, and nutmeg. Place sliced peaches into the prepared baking dish.

Sift together the gluten-free flour, and Stevia Powder, into a medium bowl. Stir in oats. Cut vegetable butter into flour mixture with pastry cutter or two forks until mixture resembles a coarse meal.

Sprinkle crumbs evenly over peaches in baking dish. Sprinkle pecans over crumbles. Next, drizzle the extra 2 tablespoons of agave over pecan and crumbles. Cover baking dish with a foil tent.

Bake at 375 degrees for 30 minutes and remove foil tent and continue to bake for another 15-20 minutes or until crumbles are golden and peaches bubbling.

Note: This recipe can be done with apples, pears, mango, or a combination of these fruits with an added 1/2 cup berries of your choice.

Gluten-free substitute: Replace oats with 3/4 cup soaked and well drained buckwheat groats. To soak groats, place 2/3 cup dry groats in 1 cup of water overnight.

Yield: Nine, 1/2 cup servings.

puddings and kantens

four apples dessert

toot for tarts lemon squares

love dove carob pudding

power pudding

think pink think thin

four apples dessert

A spiced apple kanten with raisins that taste like apple pie filling and is very low calorie.

4 organic Fuji apples
2 cups organic apple juice or cider
2 cups filtered water
4 tablespoons agar agar
1/4 cup organic raisins
1/2 teaspoon cinnamon
2 tablespoons organic lemon juice
2 droppers Stevia Vanilla Creme liquid
2 tablespoons light agave

Wash and cut apples into bite size chunks. You may peel or leave the skin on. I like to leave the skin on. Place in a medium mixing bowl. Pour lemon juice over apples and toss. Set aside.

In a medium saucepan, pour in apple juice, water, and agar agar. Over medium heat, bring to just under a boil until agar agar is dissolved and reduce to a simmer.

To saucepan add cut apples and lemon juice, raisins, cinnamon, Stevia Vanilla Creme liquid, and agave. Simmer about 15 minutes or until apples are cooked al dente.

Pour mixture into a 8 x 8 glass baking dish. Cool for ten minutes and then let set in the refrigerator for at least 2 hours.

Yield: 9 servings.

toot for tarts lemon squares

A sweet, tangy kanten made with almonds and lemons that tastes like the lemon square filling.

1/4 cup organic lemon juice
1 3/4 cups unsweetened almond milk
one dropper Liquid Stevia Lemon Drops
one dropper Liquid Stevia Clear Drops
2 tablespoons light agave
4 tablespoons agar agar flakes
1/4 cup sliced almonds, then grind in coffee grinder
sliced organic almonds and lemon slices for garnish

In medium saucepan, pour in almond milk, lemon juice. Whisk in Stevia Liquids and agave. Over medium heat, bring to a simmer and stir in agar agar flakes. Stir constantly until agar agar is dissolved about five minutes.

Stir in ground up almonds. Pour lemon and almond mixture into a 8x8 glass dish and let cool a few minutes.

Place in the refrigerator to set at least two hours. For best results, chill overnight. When sufficiently chilled, the kanten will be very firm. Cut into squares and serve with extra sliced almonds and lemon slices.

Yield: 16 squares.

love dove carob pudding

A satisfying carob pudding that tastes like chocolate and made with kuzu to sooth the stomach and strengthen the intestines.

1 cup unsweetened almond milk
1 cup water
2 droppers Liquid Stevia Milk Chocolate
2 droppers Liquid Stevia Vanilla Creme
2 tablespoons agave nectar
1/2 cup carob powder
2 tablespoons kuzu
2 tablespoons cold unsweetened almond milk
garnish: 1 teaspoon chopped brazil nuts, sliced almonds, or flaked coconut

In medium sauce pan on medium heat, bring almond milk, water, Liquid Stevias, and agave nectar to a simmer. Whisk in carob powder one tablespoon at a time until blended. Cook for 5-7 minutes stirring constantly.

Next, into the carob mixture, whisk the diluted kuzu in cold almond milk and blend until smooth. Cook while stirring constantly for another two- three minutes. Mixture will thicken into a pudding.

Spoon pudding into custard cups three quarters of the way full and chill for two hours. Cover with plastic wrap. Keep refrigerated. When ready to eat, garnish with a crunchy topping.

Yield: Four, 4 oz servings.

think pink think thin

A Japanese dessert made with agar agar, pink grapefruit, and agave.

1 cup unsweetened pink grapefruit juice
2 cups of water
4 tablespoons agar agar
2 tablespoons beet juice
3 tablespoons light agave
1 dropper Liquid Stevia Lemon Drops
2 large Texas organic pink grapefruits, peeled and sectioned

In medium saucepan, bring juice and water to a boil. Stir in agar, beet juice, agave, and Liquid Stevia. Cook for 5 minutes until agar dissolves. Set aside. Place peeled grape fruit sections in an 8x8 glass baking dish. Pour agar mixture over grapefruit. Let set for at least two hours in refrigerator or chill over night.

Yield: Nine, 1/2 cup servings.

power pudding

Dates, Brazil nuts, dark agave, and cinnamon make a great energy "pudding" and female energy elixir.

6 coconut date rolls
1/2 cup raw carob
2 tablespoons dark agave
1 packet or 1/2 teaspoon Stevia Plus Powder
1/2 cup unsweetened almond milk
2 teaspoons vanilla
2 teaspoons cinnamon
6 Brazil nuts

In food processor, puree coconut date rolls, carob, agave, Stevia, almond milk, vanilla, cinnamon, and Brazil nuts. Spoon into custard cups and store in refrigerator.

Yield: Four, 1/4 cup servings.

pizza and crackers

sweet truth pizza

polenta pizza

pizza in the raw

savory flax jaxs

fantastic apple flax jaxs

sweet truth pizza

The best gluten-free pizza crust with tomato, mozzarella, and fresh basil and a sugar-free tomato sauce.

CRUST
3 tablespoons golden flax seed, ground
3/4 cup gluten-free flour
1/2 cup tapioca flour
1/2 cup white rice flour
1/2 cup potato starch (not flour)
1 1/2 teaspoons xanthan gum
1/2 teaspoon salt
2 large egg whites at room temp
1/4 cup warm water
2 teaspoons coconut toddy with agave (vinegar)
2 tablespoons grape seed oil
1/2 cup hot water
1 tablespoon plus 2 teaspoons active dry yeast
1 tablespoon light agave
grape seed oil to grease pizza
vegetable spray to grease spatula

Place flax seeds in a coffee grinder and blend for a few seconds. Spread ground flax on parchment lined baking sheet large enough for a pizza. Set aside.

In medium bowl, sift together gluten-free flour, tapioca starch, white rice flour, potato starch, xanthan gum, and salt. Set aside.

In stand up mixer with wire attachment, whisk the egg whites until white and fluffy about 3-4 minutes. Continue beating and add 1/4 cup warm water, vinegar, and oil.

In small bowl, combine hot water, yeast, and agave. Let stand until it fizzes. Set aside.

In stand up mixer change to a paddle attachment and add pre-sifted flour ingredients to egg white mixture on slow. Dough will form small crumbs the size of peas. Next, mix in the yeast mixture and beat on high for 3 minutes.

Spray oil a spatula and scrape down sides of bowl forming dough into a ball. With greased spatula, turn out dough onto baking sheet coverer with flax seed. With spray-oiled spatula, flatten dough out to desired thickness. Medium thin is best with a gluten-free pizza. With spray oiled fingers, shape edge around the pizza to hold toppings. Cover with spray-oiled plastic wrap.

Let dough rise 45 minutes in a warm place. I like to place mine on the stovetop of a 375 degree oven with a clean dish towel draped on top of the plastic covered dough. When crust has risen, bake crust topless for seven minutes in a preheated 375 degree oven. Remove pizza from oven and top with pizza sauce, fresh basil, and mozzarella. Bake another 15 minutes at 375 or until crust is golden brown.

PIZZA SAUCE and TOPPINGS
2 tablespoons extra virgin olive oil
2 cloves garlic, thinly sliced
1 sweet Hawaiian onion, finely chopped
1 15 oz jar organic unsweetened tomato sauce
1 15 oz can organic crushed tomatoes
1 tablespoon organic tomato paste
1/2 cup light agave
1 tablespoon Bragg's Liquid Amino Acids
1 teaspoon Celtic Sea Salt
8 oz low fat mozzarella, sliced
1/2 cup chopped fresh basil
fresh basil for green garnish

In large sauté pan over low heat, add oil and lightly sauté garlic for a few minutes. Add finely chopped onion and sauté until both are translucent about 5 minutes. Stir in the unsweetened sauce, tomatoes, paste, agave, Bragg's, and salt. Simmer for 15-20 minutes and reduce liquid.

Measure about 3-4 cups of sauce and spread on prepared pizza. Add fresh basil on top. Cut mozzarella into 1/4 inch slices and place on top of sauce and basil. Bake as indicated in directions for pizza about another 15 minutes.

Garnish with fresh basil. Let pizza cool on wire rack.

Yield: One, 12-inch pizza.

polenta pizza

A polenta and quinoa crust with a purple cauliflower and roasted red pepper puree.

CRUST
1 1/2 cups water
2 tablespoons vegetable butter
1/4 teaspoon sea salt
1/2 cup polenta
1/2 cup quinoa
1 cup water
2 tablespoons extra virgin olive oil

TOPPING
1 small head of purple cauliflower
1 clove garlic
1 tablespoon extra virgin olive oil
1/2 cup roasted red pepper
1/4 teaspoon sea salt
black pepper to taste
cayenne to taste
2 teaspoons lemon juice
1 tablespoon veggie broth
organic sun dried olives for garnish

For crust: In medium stainless steel saucepan, bring 1 1/2 cups water, polenta, salt, and vegetable butter to a boil. Lower to a simmer and stir constantly until thick about 10 minutes. It is important to stir, otherwise the mixture will stick and burn. In separate small saucepan, bring 1 cup water and rinsed quinoa to a boil. Lower to a simmer, cover saucepan and cook 15 minutes.

When both mixtures are completely cooked through, add quinoa to polenta mixing thoroughly. Pour mixture into two, oil sprayed 9-inch glass pie plates. Each pie will be about 3/4 - 1 inch in height. Let cool for 20 minutes or until polenta is set and firm to touch. When cool, cut crust into triangles by first cutting an X and then a plus sign. This pattern will make eight, 3-inch triangles for each pie. Lift polenta triangles out of pie plat with a spatula and transfer to a sauté pan with the olive oil. Sauté triangles in olive oil on a medium low heat until both sides are crispy. Set aside.

For topping: Lightly steam cauliflower pieces and then place in food processor with garlic, olive oil, roasted red pepper, salt, pepper, cayenne, lemon juice, and vegetable broth. Blend until smooth, scraping down sides. Scoop onto each polenta triangle a rounded tablespoon of puree and garnish with olives and serve.

Yield: 16 pizza triangles.

pizza in the raw

Mini dehydrated buckwheat pizza rounds topped with a sauce of sun dried tomatoes.

CRUST
2 cups sprouted buckwheat
1/2 cup soaked golden flax seed
2 small garlic cloves
1 tablespoon fresh chive, finely chopped
1/2 cup carrot/beet pulp
1 tablespoon extra virgin olive oil
1 tablespoon lime juice
1 tablespoon lemon juice
1 tablespoon Bragg's Liquid Amino Acids
dash cayenne
dash sea salt

SAUCE
1/2 cup sun dried tomatoes in olive oil
1 cup unsweetened roasted red pepper
2 tablespoons light agave
1/4 teaspoon sea salt
1 teaspoon Bragg's Liquid Amino Acids
2 large Medjool dates, pitted

GARNISH
fresh chive
fresh basil
1/4 cup hemp seeds

To sprout buckwheat: Start two days before and soak 2 cups raw buck-wheat groats in 5 cups water over night. Drain groats in a colander, pressing the groats evenly up against the sides of the colander. Use a plate underneath to catch the drippings. Cover with plastic wrap and let sprout for 24 –36 hours in a cool dry, warm place. Little tails with grow the size of 1/8 inch. After groats have sprouted, measure amount of sprouted buckwheat needed.

For crust: In food processor, puree sprouted buckwheat, soaked flax, garlic, chive, carrot/beet pulp, olive oil, lime juice, lemon juice, Bragg's, cayenne, and salt. Place a large tablespoon of pizza dough onto Teflex dehydrator sheets and smooth into individual 3-4 inch in diameter pizza rounds (9 pizza rounds to a sheet). Pizza rounds should be about 1/4 inch thick. Dehydrate at 110-115 degrees for 8 hours. Remove rounds with spatula, flip to other side, and transfer to mesh sheets and dehydrate for another 8 hours. Pizza rounds can be kept in an airtight container for up to two weeks.

For sauce: In food processor, puree sun dried tomatoes, roasted red pepper, agave, salt Bragg's, and dates. Refrigerate sauce until ready to serve. Place 1 tablespoon of sauce on top of dehydrated pizza round and serve with chopped chive, basil, and 1 teaspoon hemp seeds for garnish.

To make carrot and beet pulp: Juice two medium carrots and one large beet. Drink the juice for instant energy, but use the pulp (the fiber remains that are left over) for the recipe.

Yield: 9 mini pizzas.

savory flax jax

These sweet and savory crackers are made with flax seed, pumpkin seeds, spicy vegetables.

1/2 cup organic golden flax seeds
1/2 cup organic dark flax seeds
1/2 cup organic pumpkin seeds
2 tablespoons agave
1 tablespoon organic lemon juice
2 teaspoons Bragg's Amino Acids
1/4 teaspoon turmeric
dash cayenne plus
dash sea salt
3 cups filtered water for soaking
1/4 cup organic red pepper, diced small
1/4 cup organic green pepper, diced small
1/2 cup slivered carrot, then diced
2 tablespoons minced onion
1 tablespoon extra virgin olive oil or hemp oil

To soak flax and pumpkin seeds: In medium bowl, cover flax seeds, pumpkin seeds, agave, lemon juice, Bragg's. turmeric, cayenne, and sea salt with water. Soak over night in refrigerator so that the seeds soak in all the flavor of spices.

To make flax crackers: Next day, stir soaked flax mixture to distribute the liquid floating on top. Now prepare vegetables. Tip: to sliver the carrots, use a vegetable peeler, then dice and add to other vegetables. Add the vegetables to flax mixture and blend well until all ingredients are even. Add minced onion and olive oil to flax mixture.

To dehydrate flax crackers: Dividing the mixture into thirds, pour onto three separate Teflex dehydrator sheets. With a spatula, smooth batter into a pizza-like shape until desired cracker thinness is achieved. Place in dehydrator and dehydrate for 12 hours at 105 degrees. Dehydrating time may vary depending upon your dehydrator and the desired crispy taste you want. The longer in the dehydrator, the crispier the crackers will get. At the six-hour point, use a spatula to peel off the flax crackers and flip. Dehydrate the other side.

Baking method: If you don't have a dehydrator, line a cookie sheet with parchment paper. Smooth batter onto prepared parchment and place in an 200 degrees oven, door open and slightly ajar. Bake at this low temperature for 6-8 hours. Half-way through the baking process, use a spatula and peel cracker off parchment, flip cracker, and bake the other side.

Yield: Three, 10 inch diameter sheets of flax crackers.

fantastic apple flax jax

These sweet crackers made with raisins and flax taste just like cinnamon bagel.

1/2 cup organic golden flax seeds
1/2 cup organic dark flax seeds
2 tablespoons Gogi berries
2 tablespoons organic raisins
2 tablespoons light agave
2 droppers Liquid Stevia Vanilla Creme
1 teaspoon cinnamon
1 tablespoon organic lemon juice
2 1/2 cups filtered water for soaking
1 large organic Fuji apple, pureed

To soak flax, Goji berries, and raisins: In medium bowl, cover flax seeds, Goji berries, raisins, agave, Liquid Stevia, cinnamon, and lemon juice with water. Soak over night in refrigerator so that the seeds soak in all the flavor of spices.

To make flax crackers: Next day, stir soaked flax mixture to distribute the liquid floating on top. Puree in a mini-food processor. Add the apples to flax mixture and blend well until all ingredients are even.

To dehydrate flax crackers: Dividing the mixture into thirds, pour onto three separate Teflex dehydrator sheets. With a spatula, smooth batter into a pizza-like shape until desired cracker thinness is achieved (about 1/2 inch). Place in dehydrator and dehydrate for 12 hours at 105 degrees. Dehydrating time may vary depending upon your dehydrator and the desired crispy taste you want. The longer in the dehydrator, the crispier the crackers will get. At the six-hour point, use a spatula to peel off the flax crackers and flip. Dehydrate the other side.

Baking method: If you don't have a dehydrator, line a cookie sheet with parchment paper. Smooth batter onto prepared parchment and place in an 200 degrees oven, door open and slightly ajar. Bake at this low temperature for 6-8 hours. Half-way through the baking process, use a spatula and peel cracker off parchment, flip cracker, and bake the other side.

Optional: Add 1/2 cup fresh pineapple or strawberries to apple if desired and for a more savory flavor, add 1/4 hemp seeds to mix after soaking flax.

Yield: Three, 10 inch diameter sheets of flax crackers.

ice cream and sorbet

carob ice cream

ice cream any day

way watermelon sorbet

carob ice cream

An easy carob ice cream made with frozen banana and almond milk.

ICE CREAM
2 ripe organic bananas, frozen
1/2 unsweetened almond milk plus 2 tablespoons
1 dropper Liquid Stevia Vanilla Creme
1 dropper Liquid Stevia Dark Chocolate
1/4 cup raw almonds
2 tablespoons agave
1/4 teaspoon cinnamon

TOPPING
1 tablespoon raw cacao nibs

To prepare for this treat, peel 2 ripe organic bananas. Cut each one into fourths. Place on a sheet of foil and wrap. Freeze the cut up bananas overnight.

The next day, unwrap frozen banana and place in food processor with Liquid Stevia Vanilla Creme, Dark Chocolate Liquid Stevia, 1/4 cup roasted carob, 1/4 raw organic almonds, 2 tablespoons agave, 1/4 teaspoon cinnamon. Add through the food processor's spout slowly the with 1/2 cup plus 2 tablespoons almond milk.

Puree for about one minute until batter is icy, creamy, and smooth like soft serve ice cream. Top with raw cacao nibs.

Note: If ice cream too thin, add extra banana or ice, if too thick, add extra almond milk.

Yield: Four, 1/2 cup servings.

ice cream any day

A sugar-free strawberry and banana ice cream with sugar-free fudge topping.

STRAWBERRY BANANA ICE CREAM
1 1/2 cups sliced strawberries
1 ripe banana
1 tablespoon lemon juice
2 cups cold heavy cream
1 cup cold whole milk
1/2 cup Swerve sugar alternative
1 tablespoon freeze-dried strawberry powder
2 teaspoons vanilla extract

FUDGE TOPPING
4 oz unsweetened Scharffen Berger 99% dark baking cacao
1/2 cup light agave
2 tablespoons almond milk
2 teaspoons vanilla extract

Garnish (optional)
Fresh sliced strawberries
Fresh slice banana
Spanish peanuts

For ice cream: Prepare ice cream maker according to manufacturer's instructions. Chill ice cream bowl at least six hours. In an 11-cup food processor, purée strawberries, banana, and lemon juice. Add in cream, milk, Swerve, strawberry powder, and vanilla extract. Pulse a few times to mix. Turn on ice cream machine and pour into opening at top of machine into frozen ice cream bowl that has been sitting in the freezer over night. Once mixture has been poured into frozen ice cream bowl in the ice cream maker, let machine run for 25-30 minutes.

For fudge topping: In double boiler, melt unsweetened chocolate with agave. When melted, whisk in almond milk and vanilla until smooth. Immediately drizzle over frozen ice cream and garnish with extra toppings if desired.

Yield: Ten, 4 1/2 cup servings.

way watermelon sorbet

A refreshing watermelon sorbet made with a hint of lime.

4 cups organic, seedless watermelon puree
1/4 cup filtered water
1/2 cup Swerve sugar alternative
3 droppers Liquid Stevia Lemon Drops
3 tablespoons organic lime juice
fresh raspberries and kiwi for garnish

To start, make sure your ice cream container for your ice cream maker is frozen and has been in the freezer over night or at least six hours before you begin.

Trim and cube a small, organic seedless watermelon and measure 8 cups of cubed watermelon. Add to the food processor and puree. Then measure 4 cups of the pureed watermelon and place in a large mixing bowl. You may have some watermelon and watermelon puree left over.

In separate small bowl, whisk together water, Swerve, Liquid Stevia, and lime juice until Swerve is diluted. Add Swerve mixture to watermelon puree and stir until puree and liquids are incorporated. Turn ice cream maker on. Pour watermelon mixture into spout of ice cream maker a cup at a time using a one cup liquid measuring cup. Turn ice cream maker on and let run for 25-30 minutes. Keep in the freezer.

Serve with fresh raspberries and kiwi.

Yield: Six, 8 oz servings.

entrees

hot ta ta tamale pie

lentils in a hurry

cool chick coconut curry

love it lentil loaf

minerva's marinara

manicotti mama

racey ricotta

chicken of the sea

black bean boost

gourmet garden turkey burgers

hot ta ta tamale pie

A Mexican spiced casserole with a sweet, gluten-free cornbread top.

CASSEROLE FILLING
2 tablespoons olive oil
6 one inch pieces kombu
1 medium, Sweet Hawaiian onion, chopped
2 garlic cloves crushed
1 cup cut green beans
1 red bell pepper
2 teaspoons cumin
1/8 teaspoon cayenne
2 ears fresh corn
2 organic ripe tomatoes, peeled, seeded, chopped
1/2 cup roasted bell peppers pureed in food processor
1 tablespoon organic tomato paste
15 oz can organic black beans
1/8 teaspoon asafoetida

POLENTA TOPPING
1/2 cup polenta
1/2 cup quinoa flakes
1 tablespoon quinoa flour
1/2 teaspoon salt
2 teaspoons baking powder
1 omega 3 free range egg, slightly beaten
1/2 cup Total Greek plain no-fat yogurt, or Greek style yogurt
1/4 cup unsweetened almond milk
2 tablespoons light agave
2 packets or 1 teaspoon Stevia Plus Powder
2 oz soy cheese grated

Preheat oven to 425 degrees. Boil husked corn in unsalted water for 8 minutes and set aside to cool.

Sauté kombu, onion, garlic, green beans, and red bell pepper in oil for 5 minutes. Then add cumin and cayenne and sauté for 1 minute.

With sharp knife, cut the kernels off the cob and add to the sauté mixture along with the black beans, tomatoes, pureed roasted peppers, asafoetida. Bring to boil and simmer for 10 minutes.

Make the polenta mixture in a small mixing bowl by beating egg. Whisk in yogurt, almond milk, agave, Stevia Plus. Add in polenta and stir. Add in quinoa flakes and stir.

In another small bowl, combine well the quinoa flour, salt, and baking powder. Add the quinoa flour mixture to the wet mixture and stir until blended.

Transfer the corn and beans mixture to an oil sprayed glass backing dish. Spoon polenta evenly on top. You may want to spray oil your spatula for easy spreading.

Bake for 35 minutes. Add grated soy cheese on top and bake for another five minutes.

Yield: Nine, 1/2 cup servings.

lentils in a hurry

A homemade curry, red lentil and kombu stew. Sweet, warm, and excellent for digestion and metabolism. I eat this every other week.

1 cup red lentils
3 cups water
10 one inch pieces of kombu
2 tablespoons sunflower oil
1 bay leaf
half of a cinnamon stick
3 cardamom pods
1 clove
1/2 teaspoon fennel
1/2 teaspoon garam masala
1 teaspoon cumin
1 teaspoon sea salt
pinch saffron diluted in 1 tablespoon water
5 medium carrots, peeled
1 medium onion, diced
2 teaspoons sunflower oil

Bring to a boil 1 cup red lentils, 3 cups water, and 10 one inch pieces of kombu. Simmer for 20 minutes.

To make curry, in sauté pan -- heat over medium heat 2 tablespoons sunflower oil, 1 bay leaf, half of a cinnamon stick, 3 cardamom pods, and 1 clove until clove pops. When clove pops, add 1/2 teaspoon fennel, 1/2 teaspoon garam masala, 1 teaspoon cumin, 1 teaspoon sea salt, and a pinch of saffron diluted in 1 tablespoon water. Reduce heat to low.

In food processor, puree 5 medium carrots, 1 medium onion, and 2 teaspoons sunflower oil. Add to curry mixture in sauté pan and cook until carrots and onion are translucent.

When lentils are cooked and very soft, add to curry mixture and cook down any remaining liquid. Season to taste. I usually add a few more sprinkles of cinnamon for my sweet tooth. Serve with cooked quinoa grains, white or red or a combo of both for a beautiful meal.

Yield: Eight, 1 cup servings.

cool chick coconut curry

Don't be fooled by the name, this is a hot vegetable curry dish .

2 tablespoons sunflower oil
1 bay leaf
1/2 teaspoon cinnamon
3 cardamom pods
1 clove
1 large Hawaiian sweet onion, chopped & pureed to a paste
2 tablespoons light agave nectar
1/2 teaspoon fennel
1 teaspoon cumin
1/2 teaspoon garam masala
12 oz block of firm tofu, diced or 8 oz chicken, cubed
2 cups lite, organic coconut milk
1 teaspoon sea salt
ground pepper to taste
4 strands of saffron diluted in 1 tablespoon organic veggie broth
2 tablespoons shredded organic coconut

In large sauté pan over medium/low heat, sauté in oil the bay leaf, cinnamon, cardamom, and clove until the clove pops in the pan.

Add onion paste and cook until the spices have been distributed evenly. Stir in agave nectar, fennel, cumin, and garam masala. Cook for a few minutes.

Add tofu or chicken and cook and sauté until tofu or meat is just cooked about 5 minutes.

Add coconut milk to sauté pan. Bring to a boil and then simmer for a few more minutes. Season with salt, pepper and saffron. Serve over cooked quinoa if desired. Sprinkle with shredded organic coconut.

Yield: Four, 1 cup servings.

love it lentil loaf

A hearty, gluten-free, vegetarian meat loaf made with green lentils, Aduki beans and quinoa.

LENTIL LOAF
spray oil
1 tablespoon olive oil
1 sweet onion, finely chopped
1 garlic clove, crushed
2 stalks celery, finely chopped
1 teaspoon cumin
1 teaspoon coriander
1/4 teaspoon sea salt
dash cayenne pepper
1/4 cup roasted red peppers, diced
1 large carrot, peeled and chopped
one 15 oz can of Eden organic Adzuki beans
one 15 oz can organic lentils
1 egg
1 cup quinoa flakes

TOMATO SAUCE
1 cup unsweetened sugar-free tomato sauce
3 tablespoons light agave
2 teaspoons wheat-free tamari

Preheat oven to 350 degrees. Spray oil an 8x8 glass baking dish. Set aside. In sauté pan on medium heat, sauté onion, garlic, and celery with cumin, sea salt, and cayenne until translucent. In mini-food processor, puree roasted red pepper and carrot. Add to saute pan and saute for another 3-4 minutes. Cool and set aside.

Rinse and drain beans and lentils and place in food processor with egg and onion saute mixture. Using pulse action on the food processor, blend until smooth, but do not over blend. Next pulse in quinoa flakes until blended. Spoon mixture into prepared baking dish.

Next, make tomato sauce by whisking together the unsweetened tomato sauce with the agave and tamari. Spread evenly on top of lentil loaf. Bake loaf for 60 minutes.

Yield: 9 servings.

manicotti mama

A vegan twist on my grandmother's Sicilian manicotti made with marinated zucchini for the pasta and macadamia nuts for cheese. You will prepare the noodle and cheese the night before.

PASTA SHELL
1 large organic zucchini
1 cup lemon juice
1 cup filtered water
1 tablespoon lemon zest
3 tablespoons Bragg's Liquid Amino Acids
1 garlic clove pressed
1/2 teaspoon oregano
1/2 teaspoon basil
1/4 teaspoon celtic sea salt

CHEESE FILLING
1 cup raw pine nuts
1 cup raw macadamia nuts
3 cups filtered water
1 tablespoon Bragg's Liquid Amino Acids
pinch of oregano
pinch of basil
1 tablespoon extra virgin olive oil
1/4 cup red bell pepper, chopped
3 tablespoons vegetable broth
1/4 teaspoon sea salt

For this recipe, you'll need a vegetable peeler. Wash and slice (or peel) zucchini length wise with vegetable peeler into paper thin pieces. Place zucchini in a bowl and cover with lemon juice, water, lemon zest, Bragg's, garlic, oregano, basil, and sea salt. Marinade 12 hours in refrigerator.

Rinse pine and macadamia nuts and place nuts in a small bowl. Cover with fresh filtered water. Soak in refrigerator over night. The next day, rinse, drain, and dry nuts with paper towel. Place in food processor with Bragg's, oregano, basil, olive oil, bell pepper, veggie broth, and sea salt and puree until smooth to make filling. Filling works best if chilled for two more hours.

Next place zucchini noodle flat, spread 1 rounded tablespoons of filling across noodle length wise and roll zucchini noodle like it was a small jelly roll. Top with MINERVA'S MARINARA on page 153.

Yield: Two dozen manicottis.

racey ricotta

An Italian, dairy-free, gluten-free cheese made from pine nuts, macadamia nuts, and spinach.

1 cup raw pine nuts
1 cup raw macadamia nuts
3 cups filtered water
1 cup baby spinach
1/4 cup chopped parsley
1 tablespoon lemon juice
2 tablespoons extra virgin olive oil
1/8 teaspoon sea salt
1 tablespoon Bragg's Liquid Amino Acids
1/8 teaspoon oregano
1 clove finely minced garlic
1/4 cup seeded roman tomato
3 tablespoons vegetable broth

Rinse pine and macadamia nuts through a strainer and place in small bowl covered with filtered water. Let sit over night at least 8-12 hours. When done, drain and pat dry with a paper towel.

In small bowl, place spinach, parsley, lemon juice, 1 tablespoon olive oil, and pinch of celtic sea salt. With your hands, massage lemon juice, oil and salt into spinach and parsley until a raw cook is achieved. It should just take a few minutes to see the spinach change and wilt. Set aside

Next, place the rest of the olive oil, pine and macadamia nuts, Bragg's, oregano, garlic, tomato, and vegetable broth into food processor. Blend until smooth. Place nut mixture in medium bowl and fold in spinach and parsley mixture. Chill at least two hours before serving. Best if chilled overnight.

Serving suggestion: Use a spread or dip, in a nori roll or on top of herbed flax crackers.

Yield: 3 cup servings.

minerva's marinara

A energizing tomato free Marinara sauce made with fresh carrot juice and red pepper.

1/2 cup fresh carrot juice
1/4 cup red pepper, chopped
1 small avocado
4 tablespoons organic raw almond butter
1 tablespoon tamari
2 tablespoons raw soaked almonds
1/4 teaspoon sea salt

Combine carrot juice, red pepper, avocado, almond butter, tamari, almonds and sea salt in a food processor and puree until smooth. For a thicker sauce, add more soaked almonds.

Note: It's best if you can juice about six medium carrot at home by washing, peeling, and then juicing carrots in a juicer.

Serving suggestion: You can add a little fresh ginger and/or cayenne for a kick if you are making it to go over cooked quinoa, marinated veggies, polenta or cornbread.

Yield: 1 cup.

chicken of the sea

It's raw, vegan and tastes like tuna. But instead, I use the other white meat – almonds.

1 cup soaked raw organic almonds
1/2 cup soaked raw organic sunflower seeds
1/2 cup soaked raw organic pumpkin seeds
3 cups filtered water
1/4 small sweet onion diced
1 large stalk celery chopped
1/2 roman tomato diced
2 tablespoons organic veggie broth
1/4 teaspoon celtic sea salt
1/4 teaspoon ground black pepper
1 1/2 teaspoons dulse
dash cayenne pepper

Rinse almonds, sunflower seeds, and pumpkin seeds through a strainer. Place in a bowl with water and soak seeds overnight. After soaking nuts and seeds, drain water, rinse, and pat dry before using.

In food processor, puree until smooth soaked nuts and seeds, onion, celery, tomato, vegetable broth, sea salt, pepper, dulse, and cayenne. Add a bit of extra veggie broth if need. Chill for at least two hours.

Yield: 3 cups.

black bean boost

A high protein, vegan saute of black beans and Portabello mushrooms served over quinoa.

1 cup dry quinoa grain
2 cups filtered water
one 15 oz can Eden organic black beans, rinsed and drained
2 red bell peppers, sliced
2 large Portabella mushrooms, sliced
one Hawaiian Sweet onion, diced
1 rounded tablespoon extra virgin coconut oil
1/2 teaspoon Mexican spice
1/4 teaspoon sea salt
1 tablespoon extra virgin olive oil

Rinse quinoa in strainer and add to 2 cups water in medium sauce pan. Bring to a boil, cover, and lower to a simmer for exactly 15 minutes. When done remove from heat and transfer to a serving dish.

Meanwhile, wash, cut and slice peppers and onions and add to large sauté pan containing heated coconut oil, Mexican spice and sea salt. Cook on medium flame for 3-4 minutes or until pepper and onions are translucent.

Wipe mushrooms clean with a damp paper towel, slice about a quarter inch thick and add to onion and pepper sauté, cooking for 3-4 more minutes.

Next, add rinsed and drained black beans and stir until all the ingredients are coated with coconut oil and spices. Cook for 2 minutes. Turn off flame and remove from heat.

Transfer bean mixture to serving dish containing cooked quinoa. Drizzle olive oil on top for extra flavor.

Yield: Eight, 1/2 cup servings.

veggies

beet greens and leek lampoon

you can't beet that

squash the crave puree

fennel and mushroom rush

sugar-free ketchup

sunset strips

homemade hummus and lotus chips

four yam mash

mock mashed potatoes

beets greens and leek lampoon

A surprisingly sweet and salty saute that goes great with quinoa.

1 bunch of leafy beet greens
1 large leek or 2 medium leeks
2 tablespoons extra virgin olive oil
sea salt
ground black pepper

Cut leeks across the diameter into circles. Don't use the end tips of the green stem if they look too rough. Remember, your intestines need to digest it.

Place into a bowl of water and push the centers of the circles so as to separate them allowing the sand to fall to the bottom of the bowl. When all the leeks appear clean, scoop out, place into a strainer and shake away excess water.

Heat oil in skillet and sauté leeks on medium heat for about seven minutes.

Wash beet greens and chop. Add to the leeks and sauté for another three to four minutes. Dish is done when leeks are translucent.

Serving suggestion: Serve with red and white cooked quinoa grain.

Yield: 3 cups.

you can't beet that

A sweet, beet puree that can take the place of mashed potatoes and increases digestion.

4 medium beets, cleaned, peeled, chopped into small pieces
2 1/2 cup water
1 medium sweet onion, chopped
2 tablespoons sunflower oil or olive oil
1 bay leaf
1/4 teaspoon cinnamon
3 cardamom pods
small pinch of clove
1/2 teaspoon sea salt
1/2 cup unsweetened almond milk
1/2 teaspoon cumin
2 tablespoons dark agave
pinch of saffron in 1 tablespoon water
1 tablespoon toasted sesame oil
pepper to taste

Simmer beats in 2 1/2 cup of water until soft about 25-30 minutes. When done, drain beets and set aside.

In large sauté pan over low heat, sauté onions in oil. Add in bay leaf, cinnamon, cardamom, and clove, and sea salt. When onions are translucent, whisk in almond milk, cumin, and agave. Simmer two more minutes and remove bay leaf and cardamom pods.

Place cooked beets and onion mixture in food processor and puree. Drizzle beet puree with toasted sesame oil and garnish pepper and saffron to taste.

Yield: Eight, 1/2 cup servings.

squash the crave puree

A super sweet Japanese squash puree that tastes like pumpkin pie.

one small kabucha squash or pumpkin, quartered
2 tablespoons grape seed oil
2 organic Fuji apples, rinsed, peeled and chopped
1 tablespoon organic lemon juice
1 tablespoon vanilla
2 tablespoons dark agave nectar
1 teaspoon cinnamon
1 teaspoon nutmeg
1 teaspoon pumpkin spice
1 packet or 1/2 teaspoon Stevia Plus Powder
3/4 cup organic apple cider
15 Brazil nuts, chopped

Preheat oven to 400 degrees. With one tablespoon of the oil, baste the quartered squash and place an a spray oiled baking sheet lined with parchment paper. Roast squash for 15 minutes.

Place prepared apples in a bowl and toss with lemon juice until it covers all the apples. Then toss in other tablespoon of sunflower oil over the apples until the oil is evenly spread. Stir in vanilla and agave.

In a small separate bowl, mix together cinnamon, nutmeg, pumpkin spice, and Stevia Plus Powder. Sprinkle spices and Stevia Plus over apples and toss. After the 15 minutes are up, pull out baking sheet with squash from oven and add prepared apples onto the baking sheet. Continue to roast for another 15-20 minutes.

Roasting is done when a knife easily runs through squash. Remove baking sheet and let cool. Discarding skin, scoop out squash into food processor one cup at a time and puree with half of the apple cider and 1/2 cup of apples. Repeat this process until you have pureed all the squash and apples. Add almond milk to thin if needed.

Transfer squash and apple puree to a glass dish. Sprinkle with chopped Brazil nuts.

Yield: Eight, 1/2 cup servings.

fennel and mushroom rush

An Italian roasted vegetable dish that satisfies the sweet tooth and aids digestion.

1 stalk of fennel, quartered and sliced
2 large Portabella mushrooms, sliced
2 tablespoons olive oil
1/4 teaspoon sea salt
1 tablespoon fresh minced ginger
fresh ground pepper

Remove green tips and save for garnish. Quarter and thinly slice fennel stalks. Wipe mushrooms with damp paper towel to remove debris and slice off stem. Slice Portabella mushrooms caps 1/2 inch thick and set aside.

Heat oil and sea salt in large sauté pan over medium/low heat. Sauté fennel and ginger in oil. When fennel has started to soften, add mushrooms.

Because of the meaty mushrooms, this can be a meal in itself and when served with quinoa for a vegetarian dish.

Yield: Four, 1/2 cup servings.

sugar-free ketchup

1/2 cup unsweetened, sugar-free ketchup
2 tablespoons light agave
1 teaspoon wheat-free tamari

Whisk together the ketchup, agave, and tamari. Use as a sugar-free/ wheat-free barbeque sauce or dipping sauce for Sunset Strips.

Yield: 10 tablespoons.

sunset strips

Sweet potato fries done healthy and light with a sugar-free ketchup.

2 medium organic yams, sliced length wise
2 tablespoons grape seed oil
1 teaspoon sea salt
1 teaspoon cumin
dash of cayenne pepper

Preheat oven to 400 degrees. Place sliced yams in a bowl. Drizzle grape seed oil over yams and toss. Sprinkle in salt, cayenne, and cumin.

Place on spray oiled baking sheet lined with parchment paper and roast for 20 minutes. Flip with spatula and roast for another 10-15 or until "burnt orange".

Serving suggestion: Serve with Sugar-free Ketchup (see previous page).

Yield: 8, 1/2 cup servings.

homemade hummus and lotus chips

A ginger garbanzo bean dip with lotus chips and no trans fats.

10, one-inch pieces of kombu
1 1/2 cups water
1 can Eden organic chick peas, drained and rinsed
1/2 cup organic roasted tahini
1/4 cup organic lemon juice
2 teaspoons fresh ginger, minced
1/4 teaspoon sea salt
1/2 teaspoon turmeric
dash cayenne pepper
1/2 cup unsweetened almond milk

In medium sauce pan over medium heat, place water and kombu. Bring to a boil and then simmer for 15 minutes. Then add chick peas and simmer together for another 10-15 minutes. This should cook down the water and leave a less than 1/4 cup liquid.

Because the broth from the kombu and beans contains great nutrients and minerals, keep two tablespoons of the liquid from the beans and kombu and pour into a food processor. Drain and discard the rest of broth from the kombu and chick peas, and place chick peas (garbanzo beans) and kombu into the food processor. Add tahini, lemon juice, salt, cayenne, ginger, and turmeric, and pepper.

Puree all ingredients while adding the almond milk slowly through the spout to get the consistency you want. Transfer to a container and refrigerate.

Yield: Four 1/2 cup servings.

lotus chips

A healthy alternative to potato chips made with lotus.

1 package lotus root
2 cups filtered water
1 cup vegetable broth
2 tablespoons olive oil
dash tamari
1/4 teaspoon sea salt

In a large soup pot, place in your steamer and add lotus chips with 2 cups of water and one cup of organic veggie broth and steam for 45-50 minutes. Drain and pat dry. Set aside.

In Teflon coated frying pan on medium/low heat, sauté steamed lotus in 2 tablespoons olive oil, dash of tamari, and sea salt. Sauté chips until golden on each side. Cool on paper towel and then dip in to the Homemade Hummus.

Yield: Six, 1/2 cup servings.

four yam mash

A cinnamon sweet yam mashed potato dish with Brazil nuts. A sure cure for carb cravings.

4 medium organic yams
1 tablespoon vegetable butter
3 tablespoons unsweetened almond milk
3 teaspoons tamari
2 teaspoons pumpkin spice
dash cayenne
dash sea salt
1/4 cup Brazil nuts

Preheat oven to 375 degrees. Wash and bake yams for 45 minutes or until a knife slides into yam easily.

When yams are finished baking, take out of oven and remove skins. Skins will come off easily.

Place the yam meat into a food processor along with the vegetable spread, almond milk, tamari, pumpkin spice, cayenne, and sea salt. Blend until smooth.

Chop Brazil nuts by hand or puree in a mini-food processor. Garnish with Brazil nuts.

Yield: Six, 1/2 cup servings.

mock mashed potatoes

A mock mashed potato made with quinoa and cauliflower.

1 medium organic head of cauliflower
1/2 cup quinoa
1 cup water
1 tablespoon vegetable spread
3 tablespoons unsweetened almond milk
1 teaspoon Bragg's Liquid Amino Acids
1 teaspoon chervil
dash cayenne
dash sea salt

Wash and cut cauliflower into florets. Steam cauliflower until tender about 10 minutes.

In a small sauce pan, bring quinoa and water to a boil and simmer with cover on for 13-15 minutes. When quinoa is done, remove from heat and let cool slightly and then transfer to food processor.

Add steamed cauliflower to quinoa in food processor along with vegetable spread, unsweetened almond milk, Bragg's, chervil, cayenne, and salt. Pulse to puree to consistency you want.

Serve immediately.

Yield: Six, 1/2 cup servings.

salads

nori rolls

pasta

dressings

hijiki salad

mermaid salad

rawsome awesome salad massage

tomago tuber

soba with brazil nut pesto

sunflower salad dressing

kelly's cali rolls

hold your horses hijiki salad

A sweet and salty sea weed salad for strong, shiny hairy and beautiful skin. Highly digestible.

1/4 cup dry hijiki
1/4 cup dry arame
1/4 cup walkame
2 1/2 cups filtered water
3 tablespoons toasted sesame oil
2 teaspoons organic lemon juice
1 tablespoon light agave
1/4 teaspoon sea salt
ground black pepper
cayenne
1/2 cup organic vegetable stock
1 cup lotus, thinly sliced
3/4 cup burdock, thinly sliced
1/2 cup roasted bell peppers
1 teaspoon freshly minced ginger
1 tablespoon sesame seeds

Place hijiki, arame, and walkame in glass bowl and add water. Set aside for 20 minutes. When sea vegetables have fully hydrated, drain and pat dry with paper towel. Add toasted sesame oil and lemon juice to sea vegetables and mix well. Add in salt, pepper, and cayenne to taste.

In sauté pan, heat vegetable stock and cook lotus and burdock until tender about 40 minutes. Drain off any extra liquid.

In food processor, pulse together with a few pulse actions the cooled lotus, burdock, ginger and bell peppers. In a separate bowl, add this mixture to seaweed. Stir in sesame seeds.

Yield: Eight, 1/2 cup servings.

mermaid salad

A quinoa and avocado salad, flavored with sea salt and turmeric and accented with toasted sesame oil and sea vegetables.

1/4 cup of arame
1/4 cup walkame
1 1/2 cups filtered water
1 cup dry quinoa grain, rinsed
2 cups water
2 tablespoons toasted sesame oil
1 ripe avocado
2 teaspoons organic lemon juice
1/2 teaspoon turmeric
dash cayenne pepper
1/4 teaspoon sea salt
black pepper to taste

Soak arame and walkame in filtered water for 20 minutes or until the sea weed is fully hydrated.

Next, place 2 cups water and 1 cup quinoa in medium sauce pan. Bring to a boil, cover, and simmer on low for 15 minutes. Your quinoa will come out full and soft.

When quinoa is cooked, place immediately in a serving bowl. Mix in toasted sesame seed oil, salt, cayenne, and pepper. Set aside.

Drain arame and walkame through a strainer and press out any remaining liquid. Add to quinoa and lightly toss.

Slice avocado and place on top of salad. Sprinkle with lemon juice and toss lightly.

Yield: Eight, 1/2 cup servings.

rawsome awesome salad massage

A raw salad of super greens that have been "cooked" by a lemon, oil, and sea salt massage.

1/2 bunch of dandelion greens
1/2 bunch of red chard
3 tablespoons extra virgin olive oil
juice of one lemon
1/4 teaspoon celtic sea salt
2 Roman tomatoes
1/2 cup multi-colored bell peppers
1 cucumber, peeled and sliced
1 avocado, sliced
1 cup sunflower sprouts
1/4 cup hemp seeds
dash of cayenne
1/8 teaspoon turmeric

Recipe substitute: Also can use kale and beet greens, or even mustard greens and cilantro.

Wash and dry all vegetables. Cut dandelion and chard into tiny slivered pieces and place in large mixing bowl. Add oil, lemon, and salt. With clean hands, massage lemon mixture into greens until they start to appear cooked. About 30 seconds to 1 minute. Wipe lettuce off hands and back into bowl. This is a salad massage after all.

Massage your own hands now and let olive oil soften your own skin. Rinse hands under water and wipe with paper towel.

Next dice or slice, tomatoes, peppers, peeled cucumber, sprouts, and avocado and toss into large mixing bowl with greens. Toss ingredients together. Sprinkle cayenne, turmeric, and hemp seeds on top and toss.

Yield: Six, 1 cup servings.

the tomago tuber

A Japanese nori wrap made with Omega 3 organic free-range eggs and the spice, turmeric, a beauty secret known to many natives of Okinawa, Japan for it's balancing and anti-inflammatory properties.

1 tablespoon hijiki
1 tablespoon wakame
1 tablespoon arame
1 cup filtered water
grape seed spray oil
2 free-range omega 3 eggs, beaten
1 teaspoon light agave
1/8 teaspoon sea salt
1/8 teaspoon turmeric
dash cayenne pepper
1 nori sheet
1/4 avocado, thinly sliced
dash black pepper
1 tablespoon toasted sesame oil

Soak hijiki, wakame, and arame in 1 cup filtered water. Allow 20 minutes for the sea weed to fully hydrate. When sea weed is ready, drain and measure 3 rounded tablespoons of mixed seaweed and set aside.

Coat a frying pan with non-stick spray. Scramble beaten eggs with agave, sea salt, turmeric, and cayenne. Set aside.

On sushi mat with slats running horizontal to the work area, place nori sheet, shiny side down. At edge of sheet, scoop on cooked egg and arrange into a rectangle shape on the bottom third of the nori sheet. Place sea vegetables in a line along the edge of the egg. Tuck in the avocado along of and on top of the sea weed. Drizzle sesame oil over egg,seaweed,and avocado.

Using forefinger and thumb, roll the nori over and use the mat to help keep the roll tight until you've reached the end of the seaweed wrap.

Place the roll seam side down upon a cutting board and use a wet, sharp knife to cut the roll in 1/2 inch wide rolls. Or eat like a breakfast burrito.

Yield: Six, 1/2 inch pieces.

so sassy soba with brazil nut pesto

A gluten-free pasta with the unique flavors of nori and Brazil nuts and topped with sesame seeds.

1 package Eden 100% Soba Buckwheat noodles
1/2 cup Brazil nuts
3 roasted nori sheets
2 tablespoons toasted sesame oil
2 teaspoons agave nectar
2 teaspoons sesame seeds
Sea salt to taste

Cook noodles according to package and be sure to rinse in ice cold water and pat dry. Because 100% buckwheat noodles have no wheat, they can be a bit sticky. When noodles are dry, immediately transfer to serving bowl.

In food processor, combine Brazil nuts, nori sheets torn in quarters, sesame oil, agave nectar, and a dash of sea salt. Puree until you make a pesto paste.

Spoon pesto on top of Soba noodle and toss.

Yield: Four, 1/2 cup servings.

salad dressing

A savory, sweet, and dressing made with sunflower seed butter.

2 tablespoons organic lemon juice
2 tablespoons filtered water
1/2 cup organic vegetable broth
2 tablespoons agave nectar
1/2 cup raw sunflower butter
dash cayenne pepper
2 teaspoons low salt, wheat-free tamari
Dash of sea salt

In a bowl, whisk together lemon juice, water, and vegetable broth. Whisk in agave and then sunflower butter. Add cayenne, tamari and salt. Stir and serve. Keep refrigerated. Optional: You may use organic raw tahini, almond butter, or peanut butter.

Yield: 12 tablespoons.

polenta pyramids

A gluten-free alternative to croutons and crackers using polenta.

12 oz ready made organic polenta
2 tablespoons grape seed oil
2 tablespoons agave nectar
1/4 teaspoon fennel
dash of sea salt

Preheat oven to 400 degrees. Cut polenta loaf into 1/2 inch rounds and then into quarters to make triangles and place in a bowl.

Next toss with oil, agave nectar, fennel, and sea salt. Place on a parchment paper lined baking sheet and bake for 25 minutes until golden turning them over halfway through.

Yield: 32 triangles.

kelly's cali rolls

A California roll made with nori, veggies, and quinoa.

1 cup dry quinoa
2 cups plus 2 tablespoons water
1/4 cup raw organic Artisana black tahini
8 nori sheets
2 thinly sliced avocados
2 large carrots, peeled and thinly sliced length wise
1 large cucumber, peeled and thinly sliced length wise
1/4 cup toasted sesame oil
Bragg's Liquid Amino Acids in spray bottle
sea salt to taste

For quinoa: To cook quinoa for sushi rolls, rinse quinoa in a strainer and then place in a medium saucepan with water. Bring to a boil, lower heat to a simmer, cover and cook 15 minutes. This will make a heavier quinoa, but is a good texture for the sushi roll. When done, place in bowl and let cool enough to handle.

For California roll: Place nori, shiny side down on bamboo mat covered in plastic wrap. Slats on bamboo mat will run horizontally to your work surface. On the bottom portion of nori sheet, spoon four tablespoons of cooled, cooked quinoa onto nori sheet and spread into flat 2 inch by 5 inch rectangle covering the lower third of the nori sheet. Spread about 2 teaspoons of tahini on top of quinoa.

Against the 5 inch width of the quinoa, press the cucumber, carrot, and avocado slices lengthwise. Drizzle 1/2 teaspoon of sesame oil on top and spray 2 - 3 squirts of Bragg's on top. Salt to taste.

To roll: With wet fingertips, gently dampen the far edge of the nori sheet so that the edges adhere to each other. Hold the core ingredients in place with your fingertips and use your thumbs to lift the end of the mat. The edge of the nori sheet closest to you should be lifted and rolled tightly over to meet the far edge. Briefly press the mat around the roll to set and shape the roll and seal the edges. Release the mat. Use a serrated knife dipped in hot water and cut one inch rolls like you would cut through a pieces of bread. Garnish with fresh vegetables.

Yield: 8 rolls.

30 second snacks

apple sauce & almond crumble

trail mix

spoon macaroon

vanilla low carb yogurt

applesauce and almond crumble

A quick mock apple pie with almond and cinnamon crumble.

3/4 cup unsweetened applesauce
1 tablespoon almond meal
1/4 teaspoon cinnamon
1 teaspoon light agave

Spoon out 3/4 cup of unsweetened applesauce and place in a clear custard cup. In a small measuring cup, place 1 rounded tablespoons of almond meal (Bob Red Mill's - not Trader Joe's), cinnamon and 1 teaspoon of light agave. Mix all ingredients together to make a crumble. Spoon on top of applesauce.

Yield: A one cup serving.

trail mix

Made with Goji berries and raw cacao, it's like dark chocolate and raspberries.

1 rounded tablespoon Goji Berries
1 rounded tablespoon raw cacao nibs
1 rounded tablespoon unsweetened carob chips

In a small clear custard cup, add 1 rounded tablespoons Goji Berries and 1 rounded tablespoons of raw cacao nibs and 1 tablespoon unsweetened carob chips. Mix together - eat like a trail mix. Makes one serving.

Yield: One serving.

low carb vanilla yogurt

Vanilla yogurt sweetened with agave and stevia.

1 cup plain non-fat organic yogurt
2 teaspoons light agave
1 easy dropper Liquid Stevia Vanilla Crème

In small clear bowl, add 1 cup plain, non-fat organic yogurt and 2 teaspoons light agave and 1 easy dropper of Vanilla Crème Liquid Stevia. Blend ingredients together.

Yield: One, 8 oz serving.

spoon macaroon

A coconut and hemp cookie on a spoon.

2 tablespoons hemp seeds
1 tablespoon unsweetened coconut
2 teaspoons light agave
1/8 teaspoon cinnamon

In a small clear custard cup, mix 2 tablespoons hemp seeds, 1 tablespoon unsweetened coconut, 2 teaspoons light agave, and cinnamon. Eat off a spoon.

Yield: One serving.

soups and stews

sweet lentil stew

curried pumpkin lentil soup

monday through friday soup

green goddess soup

sweet lentil stew

A sweet, kabucha squash and red lentil stew.

2 cups dry red lentils
2 one-inch pieces of kombu
3 1/2 cup water
1 cup vegetable broth
1 small kabucha squash
1 small bag baby organic carrots, peeled and washed
1 medium, Hawaiian sweet onion
2 inch fresh, organic ginger root
3 tablespoons olive oil
1/8 teaspoon sea salt
1 teaspoon cinnamon
1/8 teaspoon cayenne pepper
1/2 - 3/4 cup unsweetened almond milk
1/8 teaspoon pepper

Preheat oven to 400 degrees. Wash and sort lentils and put into large soup pan. Tear strips of kombu into 1-inch pieces and put into pan. Cover lentils with 3 1/2 cup water and 1 cup vegetable broth. Do not add salt to lentils. Bring to a boil and simmer on low heat for 40 minutes.

Cut squash into quarters, clean out seeds, and place on a baking sheet lined with parchment paper with short sides of squash face down. Thinly slice onion and ginger. Place onion and ginger with carrots in small bowl. Cover with olive oil, sea salt, cinnamon, and cayenne. Toss the vegetables until completely covered with oil and spices. Pour onto baking sheet along with quartered squash. Roast veggies for 40 minutes at 400 degrees.

Check lentils to see if soft. There should be some water left that didn't evaporate. When veggies are done being roasted when a knife passes through the squash and carrots easily. Let vegetables cool for 5 minutes and carefully peel off squash skin. Add peeled squash and add rest of veggies into a food processor. Through spout, slowly add almond milk and puree until smooth. Add pepper to taste.
Next add squash puree to lentils in soup pan.

Yield: Eight, one cup servings,

curried pumpkin lentil soup

A sweet curried pumpkin soup that is thick enough to be a stew.

2 1/2 cup water
1 cup red lentils
10 - one inch pieces kombu seaweed
1/4 teaspoon asafoetida
3 cups roasted pumpkin
1 cup veggie broth
1 tablespoon lemon juice
3 teaspoons cinnamon
1 tablespoon coconut oil
2 cloves garlic, minced
1 carrot, chopped
2 sweet onions, diced
1 stalk celery, diced
1/2 teaspoon sea salt
1 teaspoon cumin
1/2 teaspoon cayenne
4 tablespoons tamari
4 tablespoons light agave nectar
2 cups water
1 cup unsweetened almond milk
1 cup veggie broth

In large soup pan, bring water, rinsed lentils, kombu and asafoetida to a boil and simmer covered for 20 minutes. Set aside.

In food processor, puree pumpkin, broth, lemon juice, and cinnamon in a food processor and set aside.

In large skillet, sauté in coconut oil the garlic, onion, carrot, celery, sea salt, cumin, and cayenne. When veggies are translucent, add tamari, agave, and prepared lentil mixture. Stir well. Then add water, almond milk, and veggie broth. Add less water for a thicker stew.

Note: If you don't have fresh pumpkin, you can use kabucha squash.

Yield: Twelve, 1 cup servings.

monday thru friday soup

A surprisingly sweet and hearty soup for energy and detoxifying the body.

32 oz container vegetable broth
32 oz filtered water
16 oz fresh or frozen okra, cut into bite size pieces
16 oz peeled baby carrots
3 beets, peeled and sliced
1 bunch beet greens, cleaned and chopped
1 large Hawaiian sweet onion, peeled and chopped length wise
1 tbsp hemp oil
1 tbsp hemp seeds

In 8-quart soup pot, place broth and water on medium/high heat. Add okra, carrots, beets, and onions. Bring stalk and vegetables just under a boil and add beet greens. Lower to a simmer for 20 minutes. Cover pot and let sit for 1-2 hours. Instead of boiling the soup, this process will help maintain the vitamins and minerals in the vegetables.

Serve two cups of the made soup in soup bowl. Garnish with hemp oil and seeds.

Note: Use all organic vegetables.

Yield: Five, 16 oz servings.

green goddess soup

A smooth and velvety raw soup made with avocado, spinach, and kalamata olives.

2 1/2 cups organic veggie broth
2 cups fresh spinach
3 stalks celery, chopped
1/4 cup organic lemon juice
2 tablespoons miso
2 teaspoons olive oil
2 small cloves crushed garlic
7 kalamata olives
1 rounded tablespoon lemon zest
1/4 teaspoon celtic sea salt
cayenne pepper to taste
ground black pepper to taste
1/2 cup unsweetened almond milk
1/2 cup corn kernels and 1/4 cup diced tomato for garnish

To make soup: Blend the spinach with 1/2 cup veggie broth in food processor. Add celery and puree slowly adding 1 cup more of veggie broth through the spout of the food processor.

To food processor, add lemon juice, miso, olive oil, garlic, olives, lemon zest, sea salt, cayenne, and pepper and puree. Slowly add the almond milk through spout of food processor and puree. Serve chilled with garnish.

Note: Use miso of your choice. Miso found in the dairy section of the health food store and natural food stores.

Yield: Eight, 1/2 cup servings.

baby food

little people pumpkin pie

baby moose mud

mango mama baby cereal

toddler teething biscuits

little people pumpkin pie

A mock pumpkin pie filling made with Kabocha squash and Fuji apple.

PIE FILLING
1 small Kabocha squash, de-seeded and quartered
2 tablespoons grape seed oil
2 organic Fuji apples, rinsed, peeled, and coarsely chopped
2 tablespoons organic lemon juice
1/4 cup organic apple cider
1 teaspoon cinnamon
1 teaspoon nutmeg
1 teaspoon pumpkin spice
1 dropper Liquid Stevia Vanilla Creme
3 tablespoons dark agave nectar
extra almond milk for thinning if needed

TOPPING
1 cup heavy cream
1 tablespoon light agave

Preheat oven to 400 degrees. Baste quartered squash with 1 tablespoon oil and place on a baking sheet lined with parchment paper. Roast for 15 minutes.

Place sliced apples in a bowl and toss with lemon juice until it covers all the apples. Toss in other tablespoon of grape seed oil over the apples until the oil is evenly spread.

Mix together cinnamon, nutmeg, and pumpkin spice. Sprinkle over apples. Add Liquid Stevia and agave. Toss mixture until apples are covered.

After the 15 minutes are up, pull out baking sheet with squash from oven and add apple mixture to the baking sheet. Continue to roast for another 15-20 minutes or until apples have caramelized and are fully cooked.

When roasting is done, scoop out squash flesh from skin and place into food processor one cup at a time and puree with half of the apple cider and 1/2 cup of roasted apples. Remove mixture into medium bowl. Repeat this process until you have pureed all the squash and apples.

Mix together in a bowl. If you want to thin it out, add a tablespoon of almond milk. Transfer to individual custard cups.

To make whipped cream: In stand up mixer, whip heavy cream with agave until it forms soft peaks. Top with a dollop of whip cream. Eat with a spoon.

Yield: Eight, 4 oz servings.

baby mousse mud

A carob and protein packed mousse for baby and you.

one 12 oz organic Mori-Nu Silken Tofu, enriched with fiber, firm
1/2 cup roasted carob
1 large ripe organic banana
2 tablespoons light agave
1/2 dropper Liquid Stevia Vanilla Creme
1/4 teaspoon cinnamon
1/4 teaspoon xanthan gum
2 teaspoons arrowroot

ADULT TOPPINGS
3 tablespoons unsweetened carob chips
2 tablespoons sliced almonds

In food processor, puree drained tofu, carob, banana, agave, Liquid Stevia, cinnamon, xanthan gum, and arrowroot. Puree until smooth. Pour into four, 6 - 8 oz ramekins. Refrigerate for at least 2 hours before serving. Keep refrigerated.

Serving suggestion: Optional garnish for anyone who is not a baby, mix in 3 tablespoons unsweetened carob chips and top with 2 tablespoons sliced almonds.

Yield: Four, 8 oz servings.

mango mama baby cereal

A buckwheat baby cereal with mango puree.

FOR BABY CEREAL
2 mangos, peeled and cubed
2 teaspoons organic lemon juice
1/4 cup buckwheat groats, finely ground
1 cup water
1/2 cup organic apple juice
2 tablespoons light agave

TOPPING FOR ADULTS
extra mango for garnish
1 tablespoon unsweetened coconut
1 tablespoon slivered almonds

In small food processor, puree cubed mangos and lemon juice. Set aside.

To grind groats, place 1/2 cup groats in high-powered blender or sturdy coffee grinder. Grind thoroughly. Measure 1/2 cup of ground groats. You will have some left over. Put groats through a sifter to extract any pieces that did not grind completely.

In medium saucepan over medium heat, bring ground grouts, water, juice, and agave to a boil and then simmer for at least five minutes stirring constantly.

When cereal is done, transfer to a bowl and spoon mango puree on top. With a spoon, swirl puree through cereal.

Serve with milk of choice (almond, rice, soy, cow).

Serving suggestion: For adults, add fresh mango chunks on top, un-sweetened coconut, or slivered almonds.

Yield: Four, 1/2 cup servings.

toddler teething biscuits

A soft sugar-free/gluten-free teething cookie sweetened with apple juice and cinnamon.

1 cup gluten-free flour
1 cup brown rice flour
1/2 cup tapioca starch
1/2 cup instant non-fat dry milk powder
1 teaspoon baking powder
1 teaspoon baking soda
1 teaspoon xanthan gum
1 teaspoon cinnamon
1/2 cup light agave
1/4 cup grape seed oil
1 organic Omega 3 egg
1/2 cup organic unsweetened apple juice
1/2 cup ground golden flax seed

In medium bowl, sift together gluten-free flour, brown rice flour, tapioca starch, dry milk, baking powder, baking soda, xanthan gum, and cinnamon.

In stand up mixing bowl with paddle attachment, combine agave and oil. Beat in the egg and apple juice. Gradually add pre-sifted flour mixture to wet mixture. Lastly, add flax seed to dough. Dough will be sticky, but stiff. Dust hands with little extra flour and form dough into a ball. Refrigerate for 2 hours.

Fit a piece of parchment paper on a cookie sheet. Take the parchment paper off baking sheet and place on work surface. Place dough on fitted parchment paper and flatten by placing a bit of gluten free flour on top of dough and pushing down with palm of hand. Next, place a piece of wax paper on top of dough. Roll dough out to within 1/2 inch of the edge of fitted parchment. Remove wax paper carefully.

Cut rolled out dough into 2 inch by 1 inch bars. Separate the cookies slightly. Place parchment paper back on baking sheet. Bake 15 minutes in preheated 375 degree oven until light brown. Cool on wire rack.

Yield: Four dozen biscuits.

website

www.kellykeough.com

My new website is a must see for those who would like to view step by step pictures of many of the recipes, agave products that will soon be for sale, pictures of my new cooking TV show, "The Sweet Truth", on Veria network, and more info on the Sweet Truth sugar-free/ wheat-free food philosophy and food practice.